MW01031508

Romolo Augusto Staccioli

THE ROADS OF
THE ROMANS

The J. Paul Getty Museum
Los Angeles

Italian edition © 2003 «L'ERMA» di BRETSCHNEIDER

First published in the United States of America in 2003 by
Getty Publications
1200 Getty Center Drive, Suite 500
Los Angeles, California 90049-1682
www.getty.edu

English translation © 2003 J. Paul Getty Trust

Christopher Hudson, *Publisher*
Mark Greenberg, *Editor in Chief*
Robin H. Ray, *Copy Editor*
Stephen Sartarelli, *Translator*
Diane L. Franco, *Typesetter*

Giovanni Portieri, *Graphic Designer*
Maurizio Pinto, *Computer Layout and Pagination*

Drawings
Marcello Bellisario (figs. 34, 68, 88, 89)

Photographic References
Foto Giovanni Lattanzi with the exception of:
Foto Alinari (fig.s 42, 56, 76, 85, 92)
Foto Istituto Geografico De Agostini (fig.s 19, 45, 46, 72, 87, 93-95, 100)
Foto Musei Capitolini - Roma (fig.s 17, 18)
Foto Pagliari (fig.s 14)
Foto Scala (fig.s 1, 16, 20, 35, 39, 47, 53, 55, 58, 73, 74, 82, 91, 101)
Foto Staccioli (fig.s 80, 81)

Printed in Italy by «L'ERMA» di BRETSCHNEIDER

Library of Congress Cataloging-in-Publication Data

Staccioli, Romolo Augusto.
    [Strade dei Romani. English.]
    Roads of the Romans / Romolo Augusto Staccioli.
        p. cm.
Translation of: Strade dei Romani.
Includes bibliographical references and index.
    ISBN 0-89236-732-6
    1. Roads—Rome—History. I. Title.
    TE79.S6813 2003
    388.1′0937— dc21
                        2003008990

Contents

Introduction

The Romans were neither the only people to construct great roads, nor the first. The Pharaohs in Egypt and the Achaemenids in Persia did so before them, and Alexander the Great found excellent roads when he arrived in India. But the Romans, in addition to introducing technical and guiding innovations and producing numerous examples of particular importance, were able to create (and manage to optimal effect) a true *system* of roads. Rational, well-organized, and widespread—and perfectly integrated with their system of sea routes and terminal ports—this network bound together all the territories of their sprawling empire in a kind of gigantic web.

Within this great system, the roads were not reserved for sovereigns and their armies, as in Egypt, nor were they designed exclusively for commercial traffic, as in Persia. While they had been conceived in response to military needs and strategic demands, Roman roads were open to everyone, without regard for privilege or exclusivity. Free of servitude and tolls, they served the cities as well as the countryside. Over their paving stones passed soldiers, magistrates, emperors, governors, administrators, functionaries, contractors, tax collectors, and postal couriers. But every other variety of humanity used them too: merchants and adventurers, emigrants and exiles, physicians, teachers, students, healers, quacks, pilgrims, the sick, lecturers, preachers, explorers, pleasure seekers, self-educators, brigands, criminals, prostitutes, theater troupes, gladiators, peasants, seasonal laborers, free men, and slaves. And once the ancient world was eclipsed, Roman roads continued to be traveled by Germanic and Arab invaders, proselytizers and bishops on their way to the councils of the universal Church, pilgrims on their way to Rome, poets and troubadours roaming from castle to castle, students and masters heading to the university towns, popes, kings, emperors, and crusaders. They were maintained by the Gothic and Lombard kings and the Frankish and Byzantine emperors. In the Middle Ages they marked the boundaries and jurisdictions of fiefs, domains, parishes, and dioceses; along their routes, votive chapels and country churches replaced the shrines and rustic sanctuaries of the pagan epochs. Many of the population centers that sprang up around their way

stations evolved into true cities. Such, in fact, were the origins of Rome itself, which was born of a mere road or "itinerary"—the very ancient "salt route" that ran from the mouth of the Tiber to the Apennine hinterlands.

Thanks to their roads, the Romans were able to extend their conquests as far as possible; to control, organize, and manage them; to exploit them and promote their development, coordination, and integration into the empire. Without its roads, the territorial spread of Rome would never have been so vast or so exceptionally long-lasting. Commercial traffic, cultural currents, handicrafts, artworks, and raw materials traveled their routes, bringing together fashions and customs, peoples and races, doctrines, stories, legends, artistic influences, philosophical theories, religions, superstitions, inventions, and novelties of every kind. Even negative ones, as Pliny the Elder decried when he wrote: "Along what other path, if not the road, is vice so widespread? Along what other path have ivories, gold, and precious stones become so commonplace?"

In any case, it was also thanks to the roads that a broad and substantive unity was established, a union not only of lands but of men, laws, citizenship, currency, culture, art, language, and finally religion. This union took the name of Rome, and in praising the great city Pliny even celebrated, however indirectly, the unifying power of its roads: "Rome's might has given the world unity. All must recognize the favor she has done to men by facilitating their relations and interactions and allowing them to enjoy together the benefits of peace."

The ancients were aware of the important role played by the roads that Rome had built. Even before Pliny, Strabo had written (*Geog.* V, 3, 8): "The Romans have provided for three things that the Greeks, on the other hand, neglected: roads, aqueducts, and sewers." Indeed, the opening of a new road was considered on a par with a military victory or an important political initiative. It was an event worthy of being glorified and passed down to posterity. Indeed, there is no lack of actual "triumphal arches" celebrating the "birth" of a road (or the construction of a bridge, an essential element of the road); the most famous of these, erected at Benevento in Trajan's honor, celebrated the creation of the new Appian Way (FIGURE 1). And of course there are countless written commemorations set down in books or in stone, such as the *elogium* (FIGURE 2) carved into the base of the statue of Appius Claudius in the Forum of Augustus in Rome. There, after passing mention of the "many cities" the great man had taken from

APPIVS·CLAVDIVS
C·F·CAECVS
CENSOR·COS·BIS·DICT·INTERREX· III
PR·II·AED·CVR·II·Q·TR·MIL·III·COM
PLVRA·OPPIDA·DESAMNITIBVS·CEPIT
SABINORVM·ET·TVSCORVM·EXERCI
TVM·FVDIT·PACEM·FIERI·CVM·PYRRHO
REGE·PROHIBVIT·INCENSVRA·VIAM
APPIAM·STRAVIT·ETAQVAM· IN
VRBEM·ADDVXIT·A EDEM·BELLONAE
FECIT

the Samnites, his victories over the Sabines and the Etruscans, and his rejection of peace with King Pyrrhus, one reads: "When he was censor he built the Via Appia"—a road with whose construction, wrote Diodorus Siculus, "he left behind an imperishable monument in memory of himself." Eight centuries after its construction Procopius, historian of the Wars with the Goths, bore witness to this durability (*Bell. Got.* I, 14): "Once the stones were polished and flattened and cut at an angle, Appius Claudius put them together without lime or other binding material, and they now stand so united and so solidly together that anyone who sees them cannot believe that they are merely set one beside the other, but must think that they form a single whole. Yet despite all the time elapsed and the great multitude of carts that have passed over it each and every day, their unity has not been broken up in the least, nor have they lost any of their smoothness" (FIGURE 3).

The ancients subscribed to the idea of a road as a "monument" or testimony destined to endure across the ages—like the paving stones used, which were required by law to be "eternal" (*lapidibus perpetuis*). It is no accident that some roads still bear the names of some of the most illustrious and powerful families of the oligarchy that governed Rome during the Republic (the Aurelii, Valerii, Emilii, Giulii), and following them, the names of some of the most distinguished emperors: Augustus, Claudius, Vespasian, Domitian, Trajan, Hadrian, Septimius Severus.

FIGURE 3.
A stretch of the
Via Appia Antica at
the gates of Rome,
with well-preserved
pavement.

9

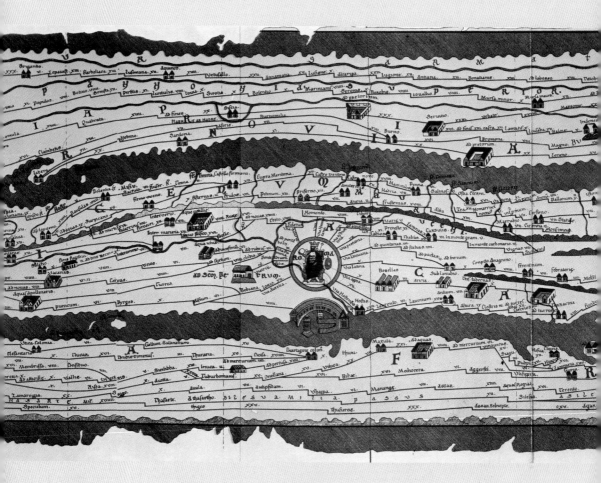

FIGURE 4.
The main roads leading out of Rome, as represented in the *Tabula Peutingeriana*, a medieval copy of a map dated fourth century A.D. Vienna, Österreichische Nationalbibliothek.

Taking stock of the entire road network built by Rome over three continents, which spans over 80,000 kilometers (over 120,000 km by some estimates), you could, as some have correctly observed, consider it the "longest monument" in the world, and indeed the longest lasting (FIGURE 4). In fact, until the end of the eighteenth century and even beyond, a good part of the European road system was still the Roman one. And this "continuation" has extended into the present time. It is therefore no exaggeration to say that Roman roads have played an important role in the very identity of Europe, in whose various languages the words for "road" and "street" are all derived directly from those used by the ancients.

The Streets of the City

I n the ancient city of Rome, which for many long centuries— before it spread into the broad plains of the Campus Martius and Trastevere and the eastern plateau— was defensively situated on hilltops and was therefore topographically very uneven, the main feature of the streets was their steep inclination. Or rather, the continuous alternation of inclines and descents—as we can still see for ourselves in the present-day Via Panisperna (along with its extension, Via di Santa Maria Maggiore), which rises and falls over the Quirinal, Viminal, and Esquiline hills. But to get an idea of how different street level is today—it has reached the point, for example, where hardly anyone walking down Via Nazionale even notices that the Quirinal and Viminal hills rise on either side—one must remember that the remains of the ancient road (the *Vicus Longus*) discovered at the corner of Via Nazionale and Via delle Quattro Fontane lie some seventeen meters below the current street level.

FIGURE 5.
Rome. Roman Forum.
A surviving stretch of
the Vicus Tuscus.

The unevenness of the terrain led the ancient Romans to use two different terms for urban roadways. Relatively flat streets were identified by the term *vicus* (plural *vici*) (FIGURES 5–6). The streets in ascent, or with many dips and rises, were identified by the term *clivus* (plural *clivi*). Still other terms were used for special cases, such as the very rare *semita*, which generically

FIGURE 6.
Rome. Roman Forum.
Remains of the Vicus
Iugarius.

means "path," "rough road," or "trail" (or even "shortcut"); or the more widely used *angiportus* (or *angiportum*), which indicates a small street, sometimes a blind alley, or more often a simple passageway. Finally, the terms *scalae* and *gradus* indicated stairways and staircases that were obviously themselves closely connected with the nature of the terrain.

Vici and *clivi* in particular bore names derived variously from intrinsic characteristics (such as the *Vicus Longus* or "Long Street"); from topographical references (*Clivus Capitolinus*) (FIGURE 7); from the presence of temples, important buildings, statues, and various sorts of monuments (*Vicus Portae*

FIGURE 7.
Rome. The ancient
Clivus Capitolinus,
still accessible today,
which connects the
Roman Forum and
the Campidoglio.

FIGURE 8, OVERLEAF
Rome. The modern
Clivo di Scauro, which
follows the same
course as the ancient
Clivus Scauri.

Collinae, Vicus Apollinis, Clivus Delphini); from the names of important people or families (*Vicus Aurelius, Clivus Scauri*) (FIGURE 8); from the signs of
shops, inns, and lodging houses (*Vicus Capitis Africae*); from the predominant
commercial activity or craft concentrating all the shops of a particular type
along a single street (*Vicus Sandalarius, Clivus Argentarius*) (FIGURE 9). Only
two streets inside the city were called *viae*, a term that as a rule was used only
for extra-urban roads: the *Sacra Via* (or *Via Sacra*), which started at the Velia

hill (not longer extant) and led west to the Roman Forum (FIGURE 10), where it was continued by the Clivus Capitolinus that led up to the Capitoline hill; and the *Nova Via* (or *Via Nova*), which ran halfway up the northern slope of the Palatine, its path roughly parallel to that of the Via Sacra. In both cases, but especially the first, the exceptional appellation is justified not so much (or not only) because they were special streets, but rather because, being very ancient, they had originally fallen outside the first expression of Palatine Rome.

In the time of Severus another Via Nova was opened to the south of the Circus Maximus concurrently with the construction of the Baths of Caracalla (though it may already have been planned in connection with the Septizodium). It ran parallel to the first stretch of the Via Appia, to which it constituted an alternative, still formally "outside the walls." Only from the end of the third century A.D., with the construction of the Aurelian Walls, did people begin to call the long stretch of the *Via Flaminia*, running between the old *Porta Fontinalis* and the new *Porta Flaminia*, the *Via Lata* (or "Broad Street"). This stretch, which today corresponds to the Via del Corso, was entirely rectilinear and became part of the city proper when the walls were built.

The streets of the "old" city—the city of the hills—were generally spontaneous in origin. This was another reason—aside from the nature of the sites—why they were for the most part short and above all narrow and tortuous. Their breadth, as decreed by law, was not supposed to be less than ten feet (roughly three meters) and on average they weren't more than fifteen. Their narrowness was also accentuated by the height of the adjacent buildings and the widespread use of balconies of various sizes and types. Only the streets of the "new" the city—that of the Campus Martius and Trastevere— were regularly based on urbanistic designs, however fragmentary and often determined by the pre-existing suburban and local "country" road system. More broad-scale planning was certainly used in the reconstruction of the city after the devastation wrought by the great fire of A.D. 64. In fact Tacitus tells us (*Ann.* XV, 43) that the *Nova Urbs* envisaged in the orders issued by Nero was supposed to have, among other things, "broader"—and therefore more regular—streets. His account is confirmed by the discontent that the realization of Nero's projects engendered: People came to miss the narrow little streets of yesteryear, which, with the help of the tall buildings casting shadows over them, "did not allow the scalding rays of the sun to pass through . . . whereas today the wide open spaces unprotected by shade are scorched by insufferable heat" (ibid.) (FIGURE 11).

Originally all the roads were cut into the ground, unpaved and simply beaten down or sometimes covered with gravel. As a result they were constantly turning to dust or mud. The first to be paved was the *Clivus Publicius*—which ran from the Forum Bovarium to the Aventine (following the same course as the present-day Clivo dei Publici)—when in 238 B.C. the two brothers and aediles Lucius and Marcus Publicius financed the project by imposing fines on illegal lessors of public grazing lands. Not until 174 B.C.

FIGURE 10.
Rome. A stretch of
the Via Sacra in the
Roman Forum.

FIGURE 11.
Rome. The Via Biberatica, lined with shops, in the Markets of Trajan.

FIGURE 12.
Pompei. Street with sidewalks (*crepidines*) and pedestrian crossing.

did the censors more broadly extend the reach of paving projects (*munitio*) and endow the streets with sidewalks (*margines* or *crepidines*) (FIGURE 12).

As for maintenance, during the Republic this task fell to the aediles, one of whom was assigned to each of the four "regions" into which the city was divided. We know that they were assisted, at least later and especially in matters of sanitation, by four special functionaries (*quatuorviri viis in urbe purgandis*). These were later replaced, perhaps in the Augustan age, by

specially assigned *curatores* (*quatuorviri viarium curandarum*). We find evidence for these officials until A.D. 260 (coinciding more or less with the end of the office of aedile), when they were called *viacari*.

Despite all these provisions, however, the problem of cleaning and disposing of the refuse that accumulated along the roads remained essentially unresolved. In the absence of a proper garbage-collection service, the streets customarily turned into veritable dumping sites. And when some kind of public intervention was actually achieved—as evidenced by the existence of *plostra stercoraria* or "filth carts"—it was only for the purpose of disencumbering the streets. There was never any question of collecting domestic refuse from people's homes. Such refuse—despite explicit bans variously formulated and reiterated over the years (and thus quite likely ignored)—regularly ended up in the street. There it accumulated alongside the garbage more or less directly "produced" by the road itself, starting with the excrement of the animals circulating in great numbers throughout the city, including horses, beasts of burden and draft animals, stray dogs, and pigs, to say nothing of the carrion and even the corpses of vagrants and homeless people or victims of ambush and murder.

Domestic waste was disposed of mostly by throwing it out the window. The practice resumed every evening at sunset. In fact, Juvenal writes (III, 267 ff.): "You are truly negligent and careless if, before leaving the house to go out to dinner somewhere, you don't first make out a will. . . . Just imagine the height from which a vase might fall on your head and break it, or how frequently cracked and broken pottery falls out the windows, leaving its mark on the pavement." Then, for emphasis: "Very often you might die for all the windows open at night along the streets you travel. Therefore work your charms and cultivate within yourself the miserable hope that the windows will be pleased to pour out only the contents of their chamber pots on your head."

But safety along the roads at night was compromised not only by the custom of throwing things out the windows. One had to be mindful as well of unlucky encounters with drunkards, bandits, prostitutes, pimps, hoodlums, and vagrants of every stripe, and the concomitant dangers of theft, assault, rape, and abduction. One of the favorite pastimes of wayward youth was to go about clubbing passersby—a custom that, according to Suetonius (*Nero*, XXVI), Nero himself used to engage in: "Just after dusk, having donned a cap of leather and felt, he would make the rounds of the taverns and wander about the streets having a grand old time making trouble, for he was in the habit of clubbing people on their way home from banquets, and if anyone reacted, he would beat him badly and throw him in a sewer." Another form of amusement, as Martial testifies (I, 3, 8), was *sagatio*, so named after the cloak (*sagum*) worn by the soldiers who originated the game and with whom it was very popular. The unlucky butt of the "joke" was forced to lie down on a large piece of heavy canvas, after which he was tossed up and down in the air until the "tossers" got tired.

The streets had no public lighting whatsoever, except on those rare occasions when spectacles at the circus or amphitheater were held at night (as we know was the case, for example, under Caligula and Domitian), or on holidays and feast days, and in these cases only circumscribed areas were illuminated. Thus anyone who had to go out at night used a torch or lantern, perhaps carried by a slave (*lanternarius*), and these sufficed barely to light one's way. Indeed, the expression *lucubrare viam* ("to light the street") idiomatically meant "to go out at night."

Another problem of the urban road system, one directly related to the narrowness of the streets (which in most cases barely allowed a single cart, in rare cases two, to pass at a given moment), was the traffic. It was aggravated by the continuous increase in the number of vehicles in circulation, corresponding to the vertiginous growth in population. The problem was resolved by a drastic measure taken by Caesar, who prohibited the circulation of carts and chariots in the city during the day. "As of the first of next January," said the Municipal Julian Law, promulgated in A.D. 45, "nobody will be allowed to use or drive [carts or] chariots in the streets of Rome from sunrise until the tenth hour [between two and three o'clock in the afternoon, depending on the season], except to transport construction materials for the temples of the gods or for other great public works or to take away demolition materials." Naturally, exceptions were provided for *ad personam* or, better yet, for specific categories of persons, but only in special circumstances: "The vehicles of the Vestals, of the 'king of sacrifices' and of the Flaminii shall be allowed to circulate in the city on occasions of sacred public ceremonies, as shall the winner's chariot and racing chariots on games days, within a radius of one mile from the city, and the chariots for parades in the Circus. Vehicles that have entered the city during the night and those equipped to transport refuse shall [also] enjoy this privilege."

By resolving the problem of daytime traffic in this manner, however, the authorities had exacerbated another: that of nighttime noise pollution. In fact, when chariots and carts resumed circulation all at once after remaining stationary in designated parking areas outside the city walls during the day, they created a deafening racket throughout the city that lasted until dawn and condemned the majority of the inhabitants to sleepless nights. One can only imagine the din made by hundreds of steel-banded wheels rolling on pavement, the hooves of hundreds more draft animals, all the loading and unloading operations, the shouts and imprecations of cart drivers, the braying of asses, the inevitable accidents, the squabbles and brawls. Not without reason, Juvenal (III, 232 ff.), thinking of those who could afford a home in more agreeable, secluded neighborhoods, wrote: "Here most sick people die of insomnia. . . . What rented apartment allows one to sleep? Only if one has a lot of money can one sleep in Rome. The source of the problem lies in the carts passing through the bottlenecks of the curved streets, and the flocks that stop and make so much noise they would prevent . . . even a devil-fish from sleeping." Martial echoes these same sentiments (XII, 57): "In the city . . . it is impossible for the poor man to fall asleep." Martial, however, does not limit himself to complaining about the nights. After all, Horace had already written (*Epist.* II, 2, 79) that in Rome, one lived *inter strepitus nocturnos atque diurnos* ("amid nighttime as well as daytime clamor"). More specifically, Martial writes (XII, 57): "In Rome, for a poor man there is no room either for thinking or for resting. The right to live is denied him in the mornings by the schoolteachers, during the night by the breadmakers, and during the day by the hammering of the blacksmiths. On the one hand there's the money-changer without clients, jingling his stock of Neronian coins on a dirty table; on the other, there's the Spanish goldbeater, striking the splintered stone with his shiny mallet; nor does the mob of those possessed by Bellona [the goddess of war] ever stop shouting. . . . The laughter of passersby awakes us, and it seems as if all of Rome is at my bedside."

Indeed, throughout the day the streets were the theater of city life, which for the most part took place out of doors. It began in the early morning hours, when they began to fill with people who actually had things to do: those on their way to work, or *clientes* on their way to the home of the *patronus* for the rite of the *salutatio matutina*, after which they went off to perform their various assignments and duties. But then there were those who, having nothing to do (as was the case for many), spent their time on the streets in search of any occupation whatsoever, or in the expectation of meeting someone who might offer them dinner. "Wandering about," writes Seneca (*de Tranq.* An. 12, 2, 4), "among the houses, the theaters, the forums, always ready to meddle in others' affairs, always with the appearance of being busy, . . . they ramble here and there without a purpose in the world and never do anything they've decided to do, but only what happens. Some arouse your pity: you see them running as if on their way to put out a fire, so furiously do they bump into those they encounter. They run to greet someone who will not return their greeting, or to queue up at the funeral of a stranger, or to attend the trial of someone with a mania for wrangling, or to the wedding of a woman who likes to rest now and then. If they run across a litter, lo, they will get behind it at once and sooner or later take the shafts upon their shoulders and carry it. . . ."

But the streets were also filled with real activities and occupations involving the widest range of people and the most disparate of tasks—from barbers to moneychangers, farriers to tooth pullers to the schoolmasters that Martial lamented, who, having not even a crawl space in which to practice their profession, would organize their classes in some secluded street corner, perhaps under the shelter of an overhanging roof or a reed mat, setting up a stool and some benches. The shopkeepers for their part, and especially the itinerant peddlers, used the streets to display their merchandise. At one point the indiscriminate crowding of the public space became so extreme that the emperor Domitian took drastic measures that were quite efficaciously recorded—and celebrated—by Martial (VI, 61): "The fearless street-peddler was stealing all of Rome from under our noses. You could no longer see a single doorway: from top to bottom they were all blocked. You, Germanicus, ordered that the streets be cleared, and now where once we saw a path, we can walk down an avenue. No pillar is surrounded any longer by bottles attached all around it, nor is the praetor forced any more to walk in mud, nor is the razor handled blindly amid a thronging crowd, and no sooty taverns clutter the street. Barbers, innkeepers, butchers and cooks can each stand in his doorway. Now this is Rome; before it was all one big shop."

Crowding, confusion, and deafening noise were the result of yet another characteristic of Rome's roads: there, amid a variegated, cosmopolitan throng, you might, as Martial observed (*Spect.* III, 10), run across a Thracian peasant from the Rhodope mountains, a Sarmatian "fed on horse's blood," as well as "those who quench their thirst at the source of the Nile," Arabs, Sabeans, and Cilicians "steeped in saffron," Sicambrians "with their hair twisted up in a knot," and Ethiopians "done up in a different style." Horace had already underscored (*Sat.* II, 6, 28) the effort required to fight one's way through the crowd (*luctandum in turba*), insulting anyone who was slow to stand aside (*et facienda iniuria tardis*). And Juvenal, even more pedantically, observed (III, 245 ff.) that "the rich man, when he has business to attend to, will have himself carried through the crowd that opens up before him; he will advance quickly over their heads, inside his spacious litter. There, during his journey, he can read, write, or rest, since, the windows being closed, one sleeps better in there than anywhere else. And he will, in any case, arrive before we do. To me, who proceed in haste, the tide of the crowd before me is an obstacle, while that following behind me like a compact phalanx, is pressing at my back: one man elbows you in the side, another strikes you roughly with a cudgel; the next one bashes your head with a board, the next with a barrel. Meanwhile your legs grow heavy with mud, your feet are stepped on from all sides by enormous shoes, a soldier punctures your big toe with his hobnailed soles. . . ."

But the dangers could be even worse than this: "Here comes a long fir-tree, teetering on a cart, followed by another cart with a pine: they wobble high over people's heads and threaten to fall at any moment. If the axle on one of those great carts bearing blocks of marble from the Apuan Alps should break, and the cart capsizes, releasing that great avalanche upon the crowd, can you tell me what would be left of their bodies? Who will find their limbs and bones . . . ?"

One nearly constant presence along the streets and roads was the shops (*tabernae*) and public gathering places, especially the "inns" and shops for buying food and drink. With their characteristic features and especially their ever-present signs, they also served as convenient, easily spotted reference points, since street numbers didn't exist. But along the streets, especially the busiest ones, or at crossroads and various other strategic points, there were other "presences" as well, such as the altars and holy shrines (*aediculae*) (FIGURE 13), especially those devoted to the *lares*, tutelary gods who protected the neighborhood. And then there were the fountains—more

accurately, the drinking fonts—usually made up of a rectangular basin with a little pillar at one end spouting water (FIGURES 14–15). These were scattered about by the tens and hundreds, allowing the population to stock up on an element that only the privileged few had at home. There were also the public latrines, which likewise became rather numerous, especially after they were reduced to the essentials: large terracotta pots or jugs taken away (and replaced) periodically by those responsible for selling their contents to wash-houses. The washhouses in turn used the ammonia to launder clothes, paying into the public treasury a tax that, in the well-known and pointed words of the emperor Vespasian (who first instituted their use), had no smell of urine whatsoever.

But what finally changed the appearance of most of the streets in the imperial age, especially after the great Neronian fire, was the presence of porticoes—with columns or more often pillars surmounted by arches or, more commonly, architraves. Their construction along both sides of the roadway in front of each building was one of several measures taken to prevent or at

FIGURE 13, OPPOSITE
Rome. Roman Forum.
Shrine of Vesta at the
entrance of the House
of the Vestal Virgins.

FIGURE 14, ABOVE
Drinking fountain
along the *decumanus
maximus.*

least impede and retard the spread of fire, as repeated blazes were devastating the city. In this way it proved easier to extinguish the flames from the roof terraces, even from the upper floors. Tacitus (*Annals*, XI, 43–44) writes that Nero promised to build these porticoes "at his own expense." And the projects that were realized, however gradually, over the first and second centuries A.D.—eminently documented by the fragments of the "marmoreal plan" of Rome from the time of Septimius Severus (early third century A.D.)— succeeded in transforming Rome, as a whole, into a "city of porticoes."

The Roads outside the City

Outside of Rome or, more precisely, outside the city walls, was a branching network of roads that linked the city with the smaller population centers scattered around it. Once rather numerous, especially in the southern and eastern quadrants, these towns were for the most part rather close by, not more than a day's journey away. The roads were thus "local" and took their names from the settlement they led to. When one route led to two successive villages, the first stretch took the name of the first town, the second that of the more distant town (which as a rule ended up prevailing). And of course, going in the opposite direction, each would have been called "Via Romana." Each such road began at a gate within the city walls. Oftentimes several roads set out from a single gate, separating immediately thereafter. Most of these were the external continuation of important city streets. Having arisen from repeated use and following very ancient routes, they were "natural" roads, in that they were irregular and tortuous, with frequent variations of elevation, dips and rises, and many turns. They long remained dirt roads, or had a summary layer of gravel on top—when they weren't cut directly into the tufaceous rock typical of the region around Rome. Over time, and as the city progressively expanded, some of the initial stretches of road, in numerous instances, ended up becoming urban streets. Some were incorporated into longer, more important streets that were developed later. Few retained significant roles in transport, but almost all continued to serve an indispensable local function within an area that had become "suburban" with respect to the great city. Thus some gave their names to gates in the city walls constructed by Aurelianus in the late third century A.D., and the very establishment of these gates confirmed their importance.

From a very early date, small sanctuaries were a common presence along the extra-urban roads. Typical among them were those situated along the first mile outside of Rome, which ended up constituting a kind of "sacred boundary" all round the city. (The city maintained direct control over them and used them to celebrate some of its most ancient and important cults.) But places of worship also sprouted up spontaneously, almost always in connection with phenomena or aspects of the landscape, and these were dedicated

FIGURE 16.
Votive relief with
footprints, wishing
the traveler a good
outcome on his
journey.

to the protective deities of the roads, first and foremost the *lares viales*, to
whom people would direct their prayers and "ejaculations," such as the one
recorded by Plautus (*Mercator*, 865): "*Invoco vos Lares Viales ut me bene
tutetis.*" ["I invoke you, Lares Viales, guardians of my well-being."] Other
gods worshiped along the road included those that protected travelers and
merchants: Hercules, the Dioscuri, Mercury, and the special "god of return,"
Redicolus, to whom one devoted, in the manner of votives—*pro itu et reditu*
["for the way and the way back"]—small tablets of marble or terracotta with
representations of one or two pairs of footprints pointed in both directions to
indicate the outward journey and return (FIGURE 16). In the imperial era, the
poet Apuleius tells us of the varied typology of the roads' holy places: "an
altar ringed with floral wreaths, a grotto shaded by leafy boughs, an oak
adorned with horns, a beech crowned with skins, an isolated rock surrounded
by an enclosure, a tree trunk carved into a human shape, a meadow filled
with the smoke of libations, a stone drenched in perfumes" (FIGURES 17–18).

Another feature of extra-urban roads that began to appear in the early
third century B.C. was the presence of tombs: at first the stately tombs of
important families, built just outside the city gates, but thereafter every manner of grave, both individual and collective, often monumental in form and
display. Lining both sides of the roadway, the tombs gave the opening
stretches of the roads (in both directions, but especially outside of Rome and
near the medium-sized population centers) the appearance of veritable "sepul-
chral avenues" FIGURE 19). And the close relationship that came to be established between the tombs and the road is shown by the frequent presence, at
the front of the burial monuments, of exedrae and benches provided for travelers to stop and rest. In fact, there were often statements addressed to these
wayfarers included in the epitaphs, asking them to show pity and respect:
for example, "Hey, traveler, come here and rest a moment . . ."; "You who
pass with an untroubled mind, pray, stop a moment and read these few
words . . ."; "Halt your steps, o stranger, if you have a scrap of pity, and shed

FIGURES 17–18.
Two sides of a votive
altar with inscriptions
wishing a safe outward
journey (*salvos ire*) and
return (*salvos venire*).
Rome, Capitoline
Museums.

a tear over my wretched bones . . ."
(FIGURE 20).

One very unusual road that did
not lead to a population center, and
whose peculiarity is indicated by its
name, was the *Via Salaria*. Born in
the pre-urban era as the "salt route,"
it connected the coastal salt deposits
at the mouth of the Tiber with
the Apennine hinterland and ran
through the natural ford (and crossing) of the river at the Isola Tiberina.
Here it linked up with other routes
(aside from that constituted by the
waterway itself) variously leading to
the Latin, Sabine, and Etruscan territories, creating a true "crossroads"
that must certainly lie at the origins
of Rome. Rome thus can be rightly
defined as a "city of roads." Indeed,
it would have been natural and logi-
cal for someone to have got the idea of securing the control—and administration—of that crossroads (and the intersection of society and commerce
that must have formed around it) by setting himself up on the Palatine hill
overlooking it all. Always considered the birthplace of the city, the Palatine,
besides offering a natural base of defense from its steep cliffs (and being far
better sited for this than the adjacent Capitoline), had a large enough area
to allow for extensive human settlement.

At the Isola Tiberina, the "salt road" divided in two: one branch ran
along the left bank of the river all the way to its mouth (*ostium*), thus taking

on the name of *Via Ostiensis* (further institutionalized when the colony of Ostia was founded) (FIGURE 21). The other branch ran along the right bank as far as the *Campus Saliniensis* (or *Salinarum*), from which it took the name of *Via Campana*.

The Via Ostiensis began at the *Porta Trigemina* in the Republican Walls, south of the Forum Bovarium, and, after passing through the narrows between the Aventine and the Tiber under the name of *Vicus Portae Trigeminae*, turned a corner and ran through the Testaccio plain. It followed the same course as the present-day Via Marmorata, at the end of which, once

FIGURE 21.
Ostia Antica. The Via Ostiensis at the entrance to the city.

the Aurelian Walls were built, it had its "exit" in the *Porta Ostiensis* (later renamed Porta San Paolo) (FIGURE 22). Eventually straightened out, renovated, and repaved along an almost entirely rectilinear route in the late republican era, it followed the Tiber's course, cutting off its many bends and running along a base of small embankments for a total of sixteen miles (23.6 km) until it became the *decumanus maximus* (major gate) of the city of Ostia (FIGURE 23).

The Via Campana started at the Sublician Bridge (*Pons Sublicius*) (and later at the Emilian Bridge [*Pons Aemilius*]) and also followed the course of the Tiber. In the imperial era, after the gates of Claudius and Trajan were built, it was replaced by the *Via Portuensis*, the first stretch of which turned away from the river just beyond the point where the *Porta Portuensis* would later be opened for it during the construction of the Aurelian Walls. It cut through the internal hills just as it does today, leaving the older road to

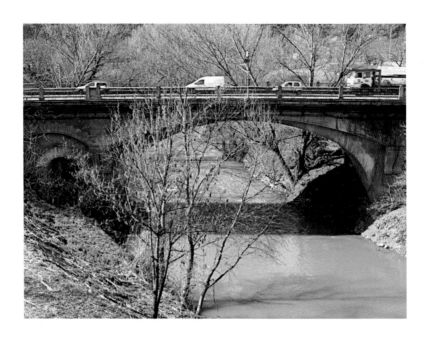

FIGURE 24.
Rome. The ancient
Pons Salarius incorpo-
rated into the structure
of the modern bridge.

function as a kind of towpath for draft animals to pull merchandise-laden
lighters up the Tiber from the port and all the way to Rome.

To return to the Via Salaria, once it had become a real *via* (we don't know
exactly when this occurred), it continued out of Rome through the *Porta
Fontinalis* on the northern slope of the Capitoline and, after having circled
round the base of the Quirinal, ascended the heights of the Pincion (following the same course as the present-day Via Francesco Crispi and Via di Porta
Pinciana). Later an alternate route was created: the *Via Salaria Nova*. This
road left Rome through the *Porta Collina* at the far end of the Quirinal, continuing northward along the present-day course of the Via Piave. Eventually
it linked back up with the *Salaria Vetus*—"old" Via Salaria—past the site of
the modern Piazza Fiume, where the *Porta Salaria* of the Aurelian Walls once
stood (whereas the Porta Pinciana served the *Salaria Vetus*). The road then
continued (as it does today) until it reached the point of confluence of the
Tiber and Aniene rivers. From here, after spanning the Aniene with the
Salarian Bridge (*Pons Salarius*) (which still survives, having been incorporated
into the modern bridge) (FIGURE 24), it proceeded up the Tiber valley to
Fidenae (near the present-day Castel Giubileo) and *Cures* (near the modern
Passo Corese). It then ran through Sabine territory to *Reate* (modern Rieti),
crossed the Apennines below Terminillo at the gorges of *Interocrium*
(Antrodoco) and, after crossing Picene territory, went to *Ausculum* (Ascoli

FIGURE 25.
Ascoli Piceno. Bridge
from the Augustan
era, called the Ponte
di Solestà.

Piceno) (FIGURE 25) and then on to the Adriatic coast to *Castrum Truentium*
(Porto d'Ascoli), 149 miles from Rome (just over 220 km).

Another unusual and very ancient road, also linked to the Tiber, was the
Via Tiberina, which followed the river valley northward on the right bank,
representing the northern continuation of the Via Campana. Later incorporated into the first leg, after the Milvian Bridge (*Pons Milvius*), of the Via

FIGURE 26.
Lucus Feroniae along
the Via Tiberina.
Crossroads near the
Forum, with a public
latrine.

Flaminia up to the present-day Prima Porta, it ran past the important area
of tufa quarries known as the "Dark Grotto," made a call at the sanctuary
of *Lucus Feroniae* (FIGURE 26), and, after crossing the Tiber, passed through
Sabina on its way to Umbria. It finally rejoined the Via Flaminia south of
Ocriculum (Otricoli). As for the commoner "local" routes, in the southern
quadrant at least two roads (aside from the Ostiense)—the *Via Laurentina*
and the *Via Ardeatina*—also led to the coast in a southeasterly direction,
linking Rome with two or three of the most ancient and illustrious centers
of coastal Latium: *Laurentum*, whose location remains unknown (whereas

in the imperial era the Via Laurentina joined the sea at the *Vicus Augustanus Laurentium*, the present-day Tor Paterno); *Lavinium* (the present-day Pratica di Mare, near Pomezia), considered the "mother city" of the Latin people; and *Ardea* (which lives on today in the city of the same name), capital of the Rutilians. The paths of the two roads (to which we should probably also add a "Via Lavinate" that would have run between them) are only very roughly followed by the present-day roads of the same names, and are more often overwhelmed by the modern streets of Via Cristoforo Colombo, Via di Decima, Via Pontina, and other smaller ones. On the other hand, several

stretches that still have the ancient paving stones are attributable to the one or the other only in certain places, and in any case, their starting points are not known with any certainty. They may have begun at the *Porta Naevia* of the Republican Walls on the Lesser Aventine, but we do know that the Via Ardeatina began, from the late third century A.D. onward, at the gate of the same name in the Aurelian Walls; this gate was destroyed in the sixteenth century to build Giuliano da Sangallo's so-called "Bastione."

Still another road must have led to the city of *Satricum* to the south (after passing perhaps through the population center of *Tellenae*). Called the "Via Satricana" by scholars, it would probably coincide, at least in part, with the present-day Via Ardeatina, which breaks off from the Via Appia at the church of Domine Quo Vadis.

Before the Via Appia was opened, an important road (later incorporated into the Appia itself) must have led to the population centers of the southwestern slopes of the

FIGURES 27–28. Rome. The ancient Via Labicana and Via Praenestina, outside the Porta Maggiore.

Albani Hills (*Via Albana? Aricina? Lanuvina?*), while another road—the *Via Tusculana*—which went out the *Porta Querquetulana* on the Caelian Hill (and later out a *posterula* [postern] of the Aurelian walls next to the *Porta Asinaria*), led to the city of *Tusculum*, just north of the modern-day town of Frascati.

Five important roads followed one after the other from north to south in the eastern quadrant, four of them originally coming out of the Porta Esquilina. After the Aurelian Walls were built, the first two—the *Via Labicana* and the *Via Praenestina*—had their own gates (with corresponding names) one right next to the other, though they were practically joined together in what became known as the Porta Maior (Porta Maggiore) (FIGURES 27–28). The Via Labicana (continued today, roughly speaking, by the Via Casalina) led to *Labicum*, identifiable with the present-day towns of Colonna or Montecompatri, and went on to join up with the *Via Latina*. The Via Praenestina (continued in a general way by the modern road of the same name) led to the city of *Praeneste* (Palestrina), site of the celebrated sanctuary of the goddess Fortuna Primigenia, after passing through *Gabii*

FIGURE 29.
Pavement of the
ancient Via Praenestina,
running parallel to the
modern road of the
same name, near the
town of Palestrina.

and thereafter being identified, in the first half of its route, as the *Via Gabina*. After Gabii it also passed through *Pedum* (perhaps the present-day Gallicano). And from this point on, for a distance over fifteen kilometers (almost 10 miles), its pavement is entirely preserved, running alongside the modern road (FIGURE 29). Also perfectly preserved is the monumental Ponte di Nona bridge (commemorating the ninth mile), dating from the second century B.C. Its seven arches are built in peperino tuff-stone, and a smaller, more ancient bridge is incorporated under the central span (FIGURE 30).

FIGURE 30.
Bridge at the ninth mile of the Via Gabina, spanning the Marrana torrent near Rome. The bridge has been known since the Middle Ages as the Ponte di Nona.

The two other roads leading out of the Porta Esquilina were the *Via Collatina* and the *Via Tiburtina*, which shared a single gate in the Aurelian Walls (the *Porta Tiburtina*, later named *Porta di San Lorenzo*). The Via Collatina led to *Collatia* (today the site of the Castello di Lunghezza), continuing on to the Ponte Lucano and then joining up with the Via Tiburtina, to which it constituted an alternate route along the opposite bank of the Aniene. The Via Tiburtina—which at an earlier stage might possibly have led out of the *Porta Viminalis*, at the top of the hill of the same name, near the present-day Termini railway station—led to *Tibur* (Tivoli) after first passing through an area rich in first-rate tufa (*"tufo dell'Aniene"*) that was mined in rather grandiose quarries from the second half of the second century A.D. onward, and then through the vast region famous for its quarries of travertine (*lapis Tiburtinus*).

Still in the eastern quadrant, there was, lastly, the *Via Nomentana* (continued today, starting from the Ponte Nomentano over the Aniene (FIGURE 31), by the street of the same name), which led out of the *Porta Collina* on the Quirinal and later out of the *Porta Nomentana* in the Aurelian Walls. After crossing the Aniene and the Mons Sacer— famous site of the pleb secession in 494 B.C.—and after passing through the short-lived village of *Ficulea* (after which its first segment, the *Via Ficulensis*, was once named), it reached Nomentum, right before the site of the modern-day town of Mentana.

FIGURE 31.
Rome. The ancient Pons Nomentanus, with medieval and modern superstructures.

In the region behind the right
bank of the Tiber and therefore in
Etruscan territory, two of the most
important roads led to *Veius* (the
Via Veientana, later partly incorporated into the *Via Cassia*) and to
Caere, the modern-day *Cerveteri* (the
Via Caeretana, later partly absorbed
into the *Via Aurelia*).

Between the local and the great
consular roads was yet another road
that was special in a variety of ways,
both in terms of its role and physi-
cal makeup: the *Via Latina*. As its
name would suggest, it can be considered a kind of "national road"
of the people of Latium, who were
definitively subdued around the end
of the fourth century B.C. and thereafter came to form an integral part
of the Roman state. It was certainly
the first road to have been "planned"
(predating the Via Appia by a few
years) and—despite being predomi-
nantly "local"—it was the first to
be extended over a great distance.
It served indeed to establish a direct
link with Capua. But it also connected Rome with a number of
other important centers along the
way, including several "colonies"
founded after the end of the last
"Latin War" in 338 B.C.: *Cales*
(the modern Calvi, in Campania,
founded 334 B.C.), *Fregellae* (near
the modern Ceprano, founded
328 B.C.), and *Interamna Lirenas*
(near Pignataro, founded 312 B.C.).
The Via Latina led out of the *Porta
Capena* in the Republican Walls
(later the *Porta Latina* in the
Aurelian Walls) (FIGURE 32) and,
partially covering some very old
routes, headed straight toward the
Albani Hills along a course roughly
corresponding to the present-day

FIGURE 32.
Rome. The Porta Latina
in the Aurelian Walls.

FIGURE 33.
Rome. Stretch of the
ancient Via Latina,
lined with tombs.

Via Anagnina. It then crossed the Albani at the Algido Pass (southeast of Rocca Priora) before heading down toward the Sacco River valley. Remaining always on the left side of the river, it passed through *Compitum Ernicum* (Crocevia di Anagni), where the Via Labicana (and the continuation of the Via Praenestina) came to an end, and then passed below *Anagnia*, *Ferentium*, and *Frusino*. Then, after crossing the Liri valley, it went through *Fregellae*

(until its destruction in 125 B.C.), *Fabrateria Nova, Aquinum, Interamna, Casinum, Teanum* (at which point a secondary road broke off from it in the direction of *Allifae, Telesia,* and *Beneventum*), *Cales,* and *Casilinum* (site of the modern-day Capua and namesake of the medieval Via Casilina, as it is still called today). Finally, 146 miles (ca. 216 km) from Rome, it reached its terminus, *Capua* (site of the modern-day Santa Maria Capua Vetere) (FIGURE 33).

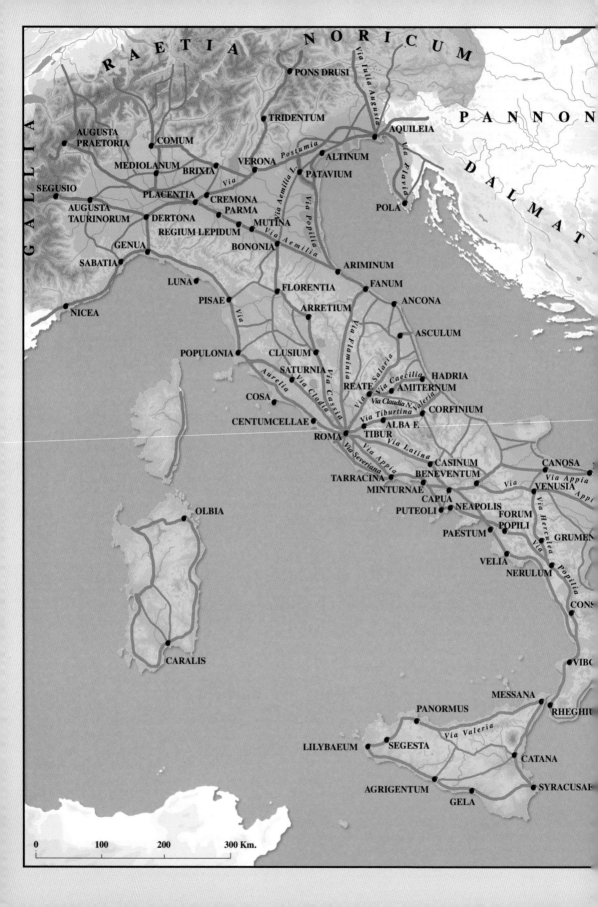

Agrigentum	Agrigento	Lilybaeum	Marsala
Alba Fucens	(Abruzzo)	Locri	Locri
Altinum	Altino	Luceria	Lucera
Amiternum	(Abruzzo)	Luna	Luni
Ancona	Ancona	Mediolanum	Milan
Aquileia	Aquileia	Messana	Messina
Ariminum	Rimini	Minturnae	Minturno
Arretium	Arezzo	Mutina	Modena
Asculum	Ascoli Piceno	Neapolis	Naples
Augusta Praetoria	Aosta	Nerulum	Rotonda
Augusta Taurinorum	Turin	Nicea	Nice
Barium	Bari	Olbia	Olbia
Beneventum	Benevento	Paestum	(Campania)
Bononia	Bologna	Panormus	Palermo
Brixia	Brescia	Parma	Parma
Brundisium	Brindisi	Patavium	Padua
Canusium	Canosa	Pisae	Pisa
Capua	Santa Maria Capua Vetere	Placentia	Piacenza
		Pola	Pula
Caralis	Cagliari	Pons Drusi	Bolzano
Casinum	Cassino	Populonia	(Tuscany)
Catana	Catania	Puteoli	Pozzuoli
Centumcellae	Civitavecchia	Reate	Rieti
Clusium	Chiusi	Regium Lepidum	Reggio Emilia
Comum	Como	Rhegium	Reggio Calabria
Consentia	Cosenza	Roma	Rome
Corfinium	Corfinio	Sabatia	Vado Sabazia
Cosa	(Tuscany)	Saturnia	Saturnia
Cremona	Cremona	Segesta	(Sicily)
Croton	Crotone	Segusio	Susa
Dertona	Tortona	Syracusae	Syracuse
Egnathia	(Puglia)	Tarentum	Taranto
Fanum	Fano	Tarracina	Terracina
Florentia	Florence	Tibur	Tivoli
Forum Popilii	Polla	Tridentum	Trento
Gela	Gela	Velia	(Campania)
Genua	Genoa	Venusia	Venosa
Grumentum	(Basilicata)	Verona	Verona
Hadria	Adria	Vibo Valentia	Vibo Valentia
Heraclea	(Basilicata)	(Hipponium)	

FIGURE 34.
The main arteries of
the Italian road system
in the imperial age.

The Consular Roads

Rome's progressive expansion over the Italian peninsula led to the creation of a new kind of road that ranged beyond the circumscribed horizon of the "neighborhood" and led to far-flung destinations. Its purpose was to solidify, speed up, and secure the links between the ruling city and the territories it had subjugated (FIGURE 34), especially the "colonies" it had established in those territories as garrisons. Such roads were fundamentally strategic with a strongly military character. However, there are plenty of examples of road projects undertaken to promote agrarian policies, which were implemented through vast land distributions in areas where it was equally necessary to improve transportation. In any case, the original military purpose of these roads was soon joined by far broader concerns, commercial ones first and foremost, not to mention the furtherance of the "Romanization" process that led to the political, cultural, and linguistic unification of the peninsula. It has thus been observed, and rightly so, that the construction of each new road constituted an event that was at once an "end" (the capture of a given territory) and a "beginning" (the start of extramilitary activities).

Even though the ultimate decision rested with the Senate, roads, because of their fundamental nature, were created by magistrates invested with *imperium*—that is, by consuls and praetors. They were the only people empowered to exercise the *ius publicandi*, which authorized them to expropriate the lands necessary for the course of the road. To be used for this purpose, the land had to be *publicus*, that is, state property. Hence they were called *viae publicae*, or "roads of the state," or also *viae consulares* or *praetoriae*. In those cases where the required land already belonged to the state, censors were also empowered to take the initiative, since their duty was to tend to the state's patrimony in matters of construction. In the imperial age, roads could be built only by emperors, who often bore the additional title of consul and were, in any case, endowed by definition with *imperium*.

Starting with the Via Appia itself, roads began taking on the names of those who built them. These names, along with those of the men who later participated in operations of improvement, restoration, and renovation, were

FIGURE 35.
Milestone from the
Via della Val Pusteria,
still *in situ*, near San
Lorenzo di Sebato,
the ancient *Sebatum*
(in the Alto Adige
region). Early third
century A.D.

FIGURES 36–38.
Rome. Milestones
from the Via Appia on
the balustrade of the
Campidoglio, bearing
inscriptions by Nerva
and Vespasian.

often carved into the "milestones" at the side of the road indicating direction
and the distance traveled or yet to be traveled. The use of milestones must
have started rather early on, since the oldest such specimen (the stone mark-
ing mile LIII of the Via Appia) was set in place between 255 and 253 B.C. by
the aedili Publius Claudius and Caius Furius. The practice must, however,
have become more generalized to the point where it became the rule around
the end of the second century B.C.: Plutarch seemed to think it worth calling
attention to the "numbering of miles on little stone columns" as one of the
road-related measures promoted by Caius Graccus in a *lex viaria* ("road law")
of 123 B.C. (FIGURE 35).

The most common form of milestone was a little cylindrical column or
truncated conical column varying between one meter and four meters in
height and ranging between forty centimeters and one meter in diameter
(FIGURES 36–38). Distances were measured in miles or, more precisely, in
"thousands of steps" and were usually designated with the abbreviation *M P*
(*milia passum*) followed by the numeral. The unit of measurement that we
call "mile" was indeed made up of one thousand steps (*mille passus*) and is
equivalent to 1,478.5 meters (rounded off to 1,480 in our calculations), since
the *passus*, at 1.48 meters, was equal to five *pedes* and the "foot" (*pes*) was
equivalent to 29.57 centimeters (rounded off to 30).

The distance recorded was normally measured from the start of the road
or from the last city passed through (and explicitly mentioned), or else from
the closest city that lay ahead. Sometimes this basic information was followed
by inscriptions of more local interest. For example, a milestone from the Via

Aemilia found at Borgo Panicale mentions not only the distance from Rome but also from Bologna and Modena (FIGURE 39). They frequently offered other kinds of information, such as the name and office of the magistrate who had ordered the milestones set in place, as well as, depending on the situation, the specific features of the stretch of road in question and the reasons for and methods of its construction or restoration. In the imperial era magniloquent texts of commemoration and celebration were inscribed on them, as is the case with one of the milestones on the Via Appia, which was restored by Hadrian. On it, one reads that the work expenses were shared between the emperor and the owners of the lands who benefited from the proximity of the road; these came to 1,157,000 and 569,000 *sestertii*, respectively. On another

FIGURE 39. Columnar milestone placed by Augustus along the Via Aemilia 79 miles from Rimini, probably at the head of the bridge over the Reno, to commemorate the reinforcement of the road. Bologna, Museo Civico Archeologico.

FIGURES 40–41.
Rome, Pons Fabricius.
The inscriptions on
the two facades com-
memorate the fact that
the bridge was built
on the orders of the
curator viarum Lucius
Fabricius in 62 B.C.

milestone from the Appia, placed there by Caracalla, one reads, among other
things: "He remade the road, which was previously ill-paved with worn,
calcareous stone, out of new flint stone, so that it would be more solid for
travelers. And he did this with his own money, for a distance of 21 miles."

Once a road was constructed, responsibility for its maintenance—*cura
viarum*—passed onto the civil administration managed by the aediles. As the
road system grew and developed, however, its management—after a brief
period in which the affected municipalities looked after them—was
entrusted to specially designated functionaries, the *curatores viarum*. This
office was institutionalized by Augustus when, in 20 B.C., he personally
assumed the *cura viarum* himself. The function of *curator* was thereafter

conferred by preference on former magistrates for an indeterminate period that could last up to ten years and more. A *curator*'s responsibility was limited either to one road, if it was particularly important, or to a group of roads, and his duties were determined on a case-by-case basis (FIGURES 40–41).

The planning and execution of roadwork were the province of specialized "engineers" usually belonging to the core of military engineers (*praefecti fabrum*), with the assistance and support of technicians of various sorts (*gromatici, agrimensores, libratores*, etc.). Cartographic aids yielded, at best, an approximation of the distances involved, especially if they were long, and the tools used for surveying and leveling were rather crude. Yet the paucity of means and instruments was compensated for by experience and great

FIGURE 42.
View of a section of
the Appia Antica.

professional skill, which allowed the road builders to lay down miles and miles of perfectly straight roads and to resume the alignment after long detours. The labor was usually furnished by the army, whose ranks provided an abundance of capable men skilled in the various requisite specialties. Moreover, using soldiers to build roads was also a way to keep them profitably busy in times of peace, and even during intervals in military operations. This is attested by Titus Livius, among others, when he writes (XXXIX, 2) that the consul Flaminius, "so as not to leave the soldiers idle, had them build a road between Arezzo and Bologna." But the practice was not very popular, as demonstrated by various episodes of open rebellion. In one such case, the legionaries of Tiberius, who were being used to build a road in Noricum, seized their commanders and forced them to work alongside, providing them with the requisite shovels and pickaxes. Prisoners of war, forced-labor convicts, and slaves could also be used—and even, when necessary, civilian laborers, who were supplied by or drafted from the communities affected by the road. On the subject of road building, Cicero, in a passage of his *Pro Fonteio* oration, writes, "All were forced to take part in the work. . . . No one was exempted."

The prototype and "grandfather" of consular roads was the Via Appia (FIGURE 42). Its construction was carried out by a censor, since the land it covered already belonged entirely to the state. The Appia was also the first

road to be named after its builder, Appius Claudius, who created it in 312 B.C. (though the second half may not have been built until 307, when Appius Claudius was consul). It was undertaken during the second Samnite War, with the goal of establishing a direct and rapid link between Rome and Capua that would allow the Roman army to get as quickly possible to the area of operations in Campania and Samnium in the warm season and to return to Rome just as quickly for the winter. The road also served to consecrate southern Latium's integration into the Roman state, as well as Campania's incorporation into the loose Roman-Campanian "federation" whose "capitals" were Rome and Capua. In this sense, the Via Appia had from the very start a strong political significance that would later increase with Rome's strategic expansion into Magna Graecia in the southern peninsula.

To fulfill these requirements, the road was designed as a "fast route" with long straightaways, the longest of which went from Rome to Terracina in two stretches (24 and 59 km, respectively) that diverged barely five degrees from each other. Before reaching Terracina, one nineteen-mile tract (roughly 28 km)—called therefore *decennovius*—was bordered by a canal that served as an alternative to the road and along which one could navigate, preferably between sunset and morning, on a barge drawn by mules along its banks (FIGURE 43). (The canal persists today, along the so-called *fettuccia*, or "little slice".)

FIGURE 43.
The canal flanking the *fettuccia* ("slice") of Terracina, a continuation of the ancient *decennovius* of the Via Appia practically unaltered since antiquity.

The Via Appia left Rome (together with the Via Latina) through the Porta Capena in the Republican Walls, skirted the Albani Hills massif, and crossed the Pontine marshes (after great reclamation efforts). East of Terracina, it spanned the gorges of Itri (and the Aurunci Mountains), descended into the plain of the Volturnus, and terminated in a last straightaway of roughly twenty-two kilometers. The distance between Rome and Capua was 132 miles (slightly more than 195 km) and could be traveled on foot in five or six days, saving fifteen miles, and therefore a day's travel, compared to the Via Latina.

At first the road must have only been covered in gravel, since the first mile—
the one that would become "urban" almost 600 years later after the construction of the Aurelian Walls, which the road pierced through the Porta Appia
(later called the Porta di San Sebastiano) (FIGURE 44)—wasn't paved
until 296 B.C. The next tract, up to *Bovillae*, was paved in A.D. 293, and the
rest followed later.

About half a century later, Rome won its war against Tarentum
and Pyrrhus. To consolidate the Roman presence between Campania and
Samnium, the Via Appia was extended as far as modern-day Benevento,

FIGURE 44.
Rome. The Porta
Appia in the Aurelian
Walls, now known
as the Porta di San
Sebastiano.

FIGURES 45–46.
Two milestones
from the Via Appia
discovered between
Benevento and
Mirabella Eclano
(ancient *Aeclanum*).
The inscriptions com-
memorate the restora-
tion of the road under
the rule of Hadrian,
and the contributions
of the local land-
owners, in A.D. 123.
Benevento, Museo
del Sannio.

FIGURE 47.
Brindisi. One of the
terminal columns of
the Via Appia, still in
its original location.

where, in 268 B.C., the Latin colony of *Beneventum* was founded (FIGURES 45–46). Then, still in the third century B.C., it was further extended across the Apennines to *Venusia* (Venosa), where a colony had existed since 291 B.C.; from here it was carried forward to *Tarentum* and finally, around the turn of the century, all the way to Brindisi. Its total length, from Rome, was 364 miles (538 km) (FIGURE 47).

After the Appia, a whole series of new road projects were launched. In addition to the above-mentioned continuation of the Via Salaria to the

Adriatic Sea, the Via Tiburtina, together with the *Via Valeria*, was extended (perhaps thanks to efforts of Consul Marcus Valerius Maximus) from Tivoli to the colony of *Alba Fucens*, above the Fucino basin (FIGURES 48–49), passing through the Aniene River valley along the way. On the Tyrrhenian side of the peninsula, after the cities of the southern Etrurian coastline were subjugated and a series of maritime colonies were founded from *Fregenae* to *Cosa* on the Argentario promontory, the Via Aurelia was laid down, probably through the offices of the censor Caius Aurelius Cotta, using and connecting already existing tracts of road. This road (which today is National Road S1) started out in Rome at the Pons Aemilius and, after an initial stretch along the right bank of the Tiber (retraced today by the Via della Lungaretta), ascended the

FIGURES 48–49. Alba Fucens. The so-called Pillar Street in the town center, and a model reconstruction of one stretch.

FIGURE 50.
Stretch of the Via
Flaminia in the
Grottarossa area
near Rome, with
remains of the great
mausoleums built at
the sides of the road.

FIGURE 51.
The Arch of
Constantine along
the Via Flaminia at
Malborghetto near
Rome, formerly con-
verted for farming
purposes.

heights of the Janiculum (where the *Porta Aurelia*, later renamed Porta San Pancrazio, was opened up for it when the Aurelian Walls were built) before heading for the coast. In the imperial era a variant of this route was created, the Aurelia Nova, which passed through the Vatican Hills before joining back up with the "old" road (the *Aurelia Vetus*, today preserved in the Via Aurelia Antica) in the suburban area now called the Val Cannuta. Initially extended as far as *Vada Volaterrana* (modern Vada, north of Cecina), the road was further continued at the initiative of Censor Marcus Emilius Scaurus in 109 B.C. into the *Via Aurelia Scauri*, which, after passing through Pisa, *Luna*, and *Genua* (Genoa), went up to *Vada Sabatia* (Vado), after which it turned northward and inland in the direction of *Aquae Statiellae* (Acqui) and *Dertona* (Tortona). The coastal route—sometimes referred to simply as Aurelia—was continued by the *Via Iulia Augusta*, built in 12 B.C. by Augustus. It passed through *Albingaunum* (modern Albenga), *Albintimilium* (Ventimiglia), and *Nicaea* (Nice) on its way to the border between Italy and Gaul, established by Augustus himself at the Var River.

On the Adriatic side, those shores were again reached when the Via Flaminia (FIGURES 50–51) was built by Gaius Flaminius, either in the year of his consulship (223 B.C.) or in that of his censorship (220 B.C.), to establish a

FIGURE 52.
Rome. Ponte Milvio.

FIGURE 53.
Remains of the
Augustan bridge at
Narni, in a painting
by Jean-Baptiste
Corot (1798–1875).
Paris, Louvre.

FIGURE 54.
Carsulae. Pavement of
the Via Flaminia at the
entrance to the city.

FIGURE 55,
OPPOSITE, TOP
Rimini. The Arch
of Augustus at the
terminus of the
Via Flaminia.

direct link with the Picene and
Gallic countryside, which had been
expropriated and divided into lots
by Rome in 232 B.C. The road
began, together with the Via Salaria,
at the Porta Fontinalis, but when
the Aurelian Walls were built, a new
gate—called *Porta Flaminia* and
later renamed Porta del Popolo—
was opened up much farther to the
north. After crossing the Tiber over
the Milvian Bridge (built much
later, in 109 B.C., by the censor
Aemilius Scaurus) (FIGURE 52),
and after a long straightaway that
continued between the right bank
of the river and the heights of
the *Saxa Rubra*, it traveled through
Faliscan and Umbrian territory,
passing through *Narnia* (Narni)

(FIGURE 53), *Carsulae* (FIGURE 54), and *Fulginium* (Foligno), which could also be reached via an alternate route over older roads that started at Narni and passed through *Interamna* (Terni) and *Spoletium* (Spoleto). The Flaminia then continued on through *Nuceria* (modern Nocera Umbra) and *Tadinum* (Gualdo Tadino) and, after the *Forulus* tunnel (Furlo), reached the sea at *Fanum Fortunae* (Fano). From there it was extended on to *Pisaurum* (Pesaro) and *Ariminum* (Rimini), reaching a total length of 217 miles (roughly 321 km). In the time of Augustus, the end of the road at Rimini was celebrated with the construction of a triumphal arch in honor of the emperor, who had restored the "world-renowned roads of Italy," as the dedicatory epigraph proclaims (FIGURE 55).

FIGURE 56.
Rimini. Roman bridge over the Marecchia River, at the start of the Via Aemilia.

After playing a decisive role in Rome's expansion into the Po River valley and more generally across the northern part of the peninsula, the Via Flaminia remained one of the principal arteries of the Roman world. This was especially true after its continuation to the Po was completed with the creation of the *Via Aemilia* (FIGURE 56). The latter road was built by Consul Marcus Aemilius Lepidus in 187 B.C., and it ran from Rimini to *Placentia* (Piacenza), passing through *Forum Livii* (Forlì), *Faventia* (Faenza), *Forum Cornelii* (Imola), *Bononia* (Bologna), *Mutina* (Modena), *Forum Rhegium Lepidi* (Reggio Emilia), and Parma, following an almost entirely straight path (as it still does today) for 189 miles, close to 280 kilometers.

Thirty years later, in 156 B.C., probably at the instigation of Censor Caius Cassius Longinus, the *Via Cassia* (FIGURE 57) was laid down, branching off from the Flaminia right after the Milvian Bridge and continuing on into the territories of inland Etruria as far as *Arretium* (Arezzo) and *Florentia*

(Florence), sharing its first ten-mile stretch with the older *Via Clodia*. This latter road (which in turn repeated much of the route of the Via Veientana) was already in place by the end of the fourth century B.C., linking Rome with the colonies of *Nepet* (Nepi) and *Sutrium* (Sutri). It was later extended, first as far as Tuscania, then to *Saturnia* and *Russulae* in the Grosseto province, and finally to the point where it rejoined the Aurelia in the vicinity of *Velutonia*.

In northern Italy, the transport axis of the Po valley took shape after completion of the Via Aemilia. The entire road system of the region eventually branched out from it, and it later led to the trans-Alpine roads as well. It was called the *Via Postumia*, initiated by Consul Spurius Postumius Albinus in 148 B.C., and it ran from the Gulf of Genoa to the Gulf of Venice. The road began at Genoa, passed through the Polcevera and Scrivia valleys, stopped at *Libarna* (Serravalle) and Tortona and, continuing on the right bank of the Po through Stradella, it headed toward Piacenza, where it intersected the Via Aemilia and continued on toward Cremona. Then, after crossing the Po, it

FIGURE 57.
Tract of the ancient
Via Cassia, alongside
the modern road of
the same name, in
the Valle di Baccano
near Rome.

began a stretch to the north of the river before forking at *Betriacum* (modern
Calvatone): one branch headed toward *Hostilia* (Ostiglia), passing through
Mantua on the way; the other—which was the more important road and
proceeded for long stretches through low, marshy land on embankments
bordered by ditches—passed through Verona, *Vicetia* (Vicenza), *Tarvisium*
(Treviso), *Opitergium* (Oderzo), and *Concordia*, before finally reaching
Aquileia. Also terminating at Aquileia, after coming up the Adriatic coast,
were two roads that alternately continued each other and conjoined: the
Via Popilia, built in 132 B.C. by Consul Caius Popilius Laenas, and the *Via
Annia*, opened in 131 B.C. by Praetor Titus Annius Rufus. They both started
at Rimini and, after crossing the difficult Po River delta, passed through
Altinum and Concordia, joining up with the Via Postumia. Before reaching
Via Postumia, it linked up at Padua with the *Via Aemilia Lepidi* (built in
175 B.C. by Marcus Aemilius Lepidus), which arrived from Bologna by way
of *Hostilia* and *Ateste* (Este).

In the south of Italy, also at the behest of Consul Popilius Laenas in
132 B.C., a second and more important *Via Popilia* was opened, which became
the major road axis on the Tyrrhenian side of the southern peninsula. It
set out from Capua (and therefore from the Via Appia), and, after passing
through Nola, *Eburum* (Eboli), the Vallo di Diano, and *Forum Popilii*
(modern Polla) (FIGURE 58), reached the elevated Crati valley. From there
it proceeded on through *Cosentia* (Cosenza) and *Hipponium* (Vibo Valenza)
before coming to an end at *Rhegium* (Reggio) after a total of 320 miles
(473 km). Its coastal alternate route, which ran from the Gulf of Naples to the
Gulf of Sant'Eufemia, later became an extension of the *Via Domitiana*, built
in A.D. 95 by the emperor who gave it its name. This road broke off from the
Appia at *Sinuessa* (near the present-day Mondragone), passing through the
marshy lands of the lower Volturno and the towns of *Liternum* and *Cuma*,
before reaching the port town of *Puteoli* (Pozzuoli) and ending at Naples.

Another coastal road, the *Via Severiana*, was created along the Latium
seaboard from Ostia to Terracina at the start of the third century A.D. by the
emperor Septimius Severus. From Terracina to Formia, by way of Sperlonga
and Gaeta, ran the road that today we call the *Via Flacca* (but whose real
name must have been the Via Valeria), almost certainly created by the censor
Lucius Valerius Flaccus in 184 B.C. to connect the port of Terracina with the
fertile land of Fondi. This region was famous for its Cecubus and Fundanus
wines, which were widely exported.

FIGURES 60–66.
Tablets carved into
the rock of the Pesco
Montano and indicat-
ing the dimensions of
the cut in Roman feet.

In A.D. 109, the emperor Trajan modified the Via Appia in two ways.
On the one hand, just outside of Terracina, the rocky promontory of Pesco
Montano (FIGURE 59), whose sheer drop into the sea forced the road to make
a long and tiresome detour by way of Itri, was cut down (FIGURES 60–66).
On the other, a true alternative to the road's long southern stretch was
created, shortening the distance to the terminus at Brindisi. The new road,
which was called the *Appia Traiana*—but which in reality was a restoration
and improvement of the old *Via Minucia*, probably opened in 221 B.C. by the

FIGURE 67.
Potenza. Roman
bridge near the city.

consul Marcus Minucius Rufus—left the old road behind at Benevento,
where a triumphal arch in the emperor's honor, still standing, was built to
commemorate the event. After climbing the Apennines and crossing the
Daunia mountains by way of *Herdoniae* and *Canusium* (Canosa), then
descending into the territory of Bari, it finally reached the coast at *Egnathia*
before continuing briefly on to its terminus at Brindisi.

In central Italy, a number of intermediate roads (or "defensive" roads with
respect to the main ones) were also built to create cross-links. We already
mentioned the *Via Clodia* and its relationship to the *Via Cassia*. Two other
roads also branched off from the Cassia, starting at Florence: one, on the
eastern side, joined up with the Via Emilia at Faenza; the other, on the western side, linked with the Aurelia at Pisa. Also bearing off from the Cassia
was the *Via Flaminia minor*, built by the consul Gaius Flaminius Nepos
in 187 B.C., which went from Arezzo to Bologna by way of Pratomagno,
Florence, *Pistoriae* (Pistoia), and the Reno valley.

Well to the south, in the heart of the Abruzzian Apennines, the *Via Caecilia*, attributed to Consul Lucius Cecilius Metellus in 117 B.C., broke away from the Via Salaria just before Rieti (or perhaps at Antrodoco) and, after passing through *Amiternum* (near the modern town of L'Aquila) and the Teramo region, arrived in *Hatria* (Atri) and perhaps went all the way to *Castrum Novum* (Giulianova) on the Adriatic. Along its first leg as far as Amiternum, it was incorporated into the *Via Claudia Nova*, which was built by the emperor Claudius to join the Via Salaria with the Via Valeria at *Corfinium* (Corfinio). Still farther south, finally, the *Via Herculia*, created by the emperor Maximian Herculius, linked the Via Popilia with the Appia from *Nerulum* to Venosa, passing through *Grumentum* and *Potentia* (Potenza) (FIGURE 67).

In northern Italy, after the sub-Alpine valleys were finally conquered in the Augustan era, the time came to build roads that would head out from the plain, in effect from the Via Postumia, toward the Alpine passes, thus creating the conditions for Roman expansion into the heart of Europe. On the western side, there was already a road—now called the *Via Fulvia*, because it is probably attributable, at least as far as its first tract is concerned, to the consul Marcus Fulvius Flaccus in 125 B.C.—that went from Tortona to *Hasta* (Asti) and *Forum Fulvii* (today Villa del Foro, a suburb of Alessandria); it was then extended to *Augusta Taurinorum* (Turin)—also the destination of an alternate route that passed through Monferrato—and continued on through the Susa Valley all the way to Monginevro. Elsewhere in the north, another long road started at Cremona, then forked into two branches—the first heading toward *Laus Pompeia* (Lodi), *Mediolanum* (Milan), and *Novaria* (Novara), the second toward *Ticinum* (Pavia) and the Lomellina region— before coming back together at *Vercellae* (Vercelli) and continuing on toward *Eporedia* (Ivrea) and *Augusta Praetoria* (Aosta). From here, a smaller offshoot went on to the Little St. Bernard Pass, while a more important artery went to the Great St. Bernard Pass.

In the central sector, one road started in Milan, passed through *Comum* (Como)—meeting another road that came from Verona by way of *Brixia* (Brescia) and *Bergomum* (Bergamo)—then took the "lake route" (*Lacus Larius*) to the Splugen Pass. Another important road from Verona went up the Adige Valley, passed through *Tridentum* (Trento) and *Pons Drusi* (Bolzano), then divided, with one branch reaching the Resia Pass by way of the Val Venosta, and the other reaching the Brenner Pass via the Valle Isarco. This might have been the *Via Claudia*, planned by Drusus the Elder (Drusus Claudius Nero), whose undertakings in 15 B.C., together with those of his brother Tiberius, had "made the Alps passable," as it was said. Restored and reinforced in A.D. 47 by Drusus's son, the emperor Claudius, the road thus took on the additional name of *Augusta*. It is more likely, however, that the real *Via Claudia Augusta* was the road that started at Altino and ended at Trento, passing through the Piave Valley and *Feltria* (Feltre), where one off- shoot went on to *Bellunum* (Belluno) before crossing the Cadore region and terminating at the Monte Croce Comelico Pass.

On the eastern side, three roads set out from the strategic center of Aquileia. One, the *Via Iulia Augusta*, headed north through the Friuli region, past *Iulium Carnicum* (near the present-day Zuglio), before reaching the Monte Croce Carnico Pass. Another headed east, through the Frigidus (Vipava) valley toward *Emona* (modern Ljubljana). The third, built in A.D. 78 by the emperor Vespasian and therefore called the Via Flavia, went to *Tergeste* (Trieste) before continuing along the western half of Istria, passing through *Parentium* (Parenzo), Pula, and *Nesactium* (modern Nesazio), finally ending up at *Tarsatica* (Rijeka).

As for Sicily and Sardinia, before the late third century A.D. they were not considered part of Italy, retaining instead, like Corsica, the status of provinces. They essentially each had a coastal road connected by internal transverse routes. In Sicily, a single road, built in A.D. 210 by Consul Marcus Valerius Levinus, started at Messina and circled the entire island under the name of Via Valeria except at the eastern end, where it was called the *Via Pompeia*.

The Great Roads of the Empire

Outside of Italy, the first great roads built by Rome in the conquered territories all began in Italy and therefore in Rome itself (FIGURE 68, pages 84–85). In fact, when Augustus took on the title of "superintendent of roads" (*curator viarum*) in 20 B.C., he had a column erected in the Forum representing "mile zero," that is, the starting point of the entire road system of the empire. On this column, in gilt bronze letters—for which the monument was called the *miliarium aureum* (the "golden milestone") (FIGURE 69)— were written the distances to all the major cities from the imperial capital. Unfortunately all that remains of this "monument to the Roman road" is a fragment of the marble base decorated with palmettes, more or less at the original site, in front of the Temple of Saturn (FIGURE 70). This was hardly an accidental location, since if one started from there and continued along one of the main axes of the *Vicus Iugarius*, the *Clivus Argentarius*, or the *Via Sacra*, always following the course of a Roman road (and being ferried, if necessary, across a brief stretch of sea), one could reach any corner of the empire. One need hardly point out that every one of these roads reflected the very history of Rome's conquests; that the entire road system was the fruit of an organic, rational design, applied with method and perseverance, and the result of tremendous effort; and that the existence of this very system, and its efficiency, were indispensable to the control, administration, and defense of an empire spanning three continents.

As if to stress the importance and right of "primogeniture" of the Via Appia—called *regina viarum* ("the queen of roads") by the poet Statius in the first century B.C.—the first road built by Rome outside of Italy was a "continuation" of the Appia across the Adriatic Sea: the *Via Aegnatia*, created around 130 B.C. by the proconsul Gnaius Aegnatius by incorporating and joining pre-existing routes. The road began at *Apollonia*, right in front of Brindisi, and then ran straight from *Dyrrhachium* (*Durrës*) on the coast of Epirus, through Macedonia, to *Thessalonica* (Salonika) in Greece. It then continued on to Philippi and along the Thracian coast, heading up the

HIBERNIA

BRITANNIA

VALLUM HADRIANI

DEVA

LONDINIUM

Rhenus

GERMANI

COLONIA AGRIPPINA

BAGACUM

AUGUSTA
TREVIRORUM

MOGONTIACUM

AUGUSTA
VINDELICORUM

ROTOMAGUS

CARNUNTU

CAESARODUNUM

AUGUSTODUNUM

GALLIA

MEDIOLANUM

AQUILEIA

EMONA

LUGDUNUM

ITALIA

ARIMINUM

BURDIGALA

NARBO
MARTIUS

ARELATE

ROMA

CAPUA

ASTURICA

TARRACO

BRACARA
AUGUSTA

CAESARAUGUSTA

HISPANIA

M
A
R
E

PANORMUS

SICILIA

EMERITA
AUGUSTA

OLISIPO

NOVA
CARTHAGO

HIPPO REGIUS

CARTHAGO

HISPALIS

CAESAREA

GADES

LAMBAESIS

THEVESTE

BANASA

LE

0   500 Km.

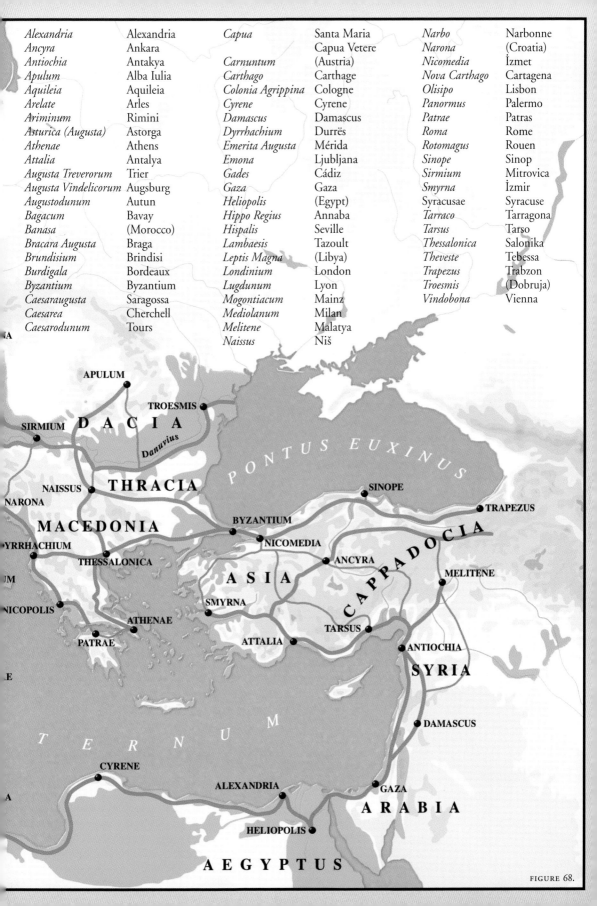

Alexandria	Alexandria	*Capua*	Santa Maria	*Narbo*	Narbonne
Ancyra	Ankara		Capua Vetere	*Narona*	(Croatia)
Antiochia	Antakya	*Carnuntum*	(Austria)	*Nicomedia*	İzmet
Apulum	Alba Iulia	*Carthago*	Carthage	*Nova Carthago*	Cartagena
Aquileia	Aquileia	*Colonia Agrippina*	Cologne	*Olisipo*	Lisbon
Arelate	Arles	*Cyrene*	Cyrene	*Panormus*	Palermo
Ariminum	Rimini	*Damascus*	Damascus	*Patrae*	Patras
Asturica (Augusta)	Astorga	*Dyrrhachium*	Durrës	*Roma*	Rome
Athenae	Athens	*Emerita Augusta*	Mérida	*Rotomagus*	Rouen
Attalia	Antalya	*Emona*	Ljubljana	*Sinope*	Sinop
Augusta Treverorum	Trier	*Gades*	Cádiz	*Sirmium*	Mitrovica
Augusta Vindelicorum	Augsburg	*Gaza*	Gaza	*Smyrna*	İzmir
Augustodunum	Autun	*Heliopolis*	(Egypt)	Syracusae	Syracuse
Bagacum	Bavay	*Hippo Regius*	Annaba	*Tarraco*	Tarragona
Banasa	(Morocco)	*Hispalis*	Seville	*Tarsus*	Tarso
Bracara Augusta	Braga	*Lambaesis*	Tazoult	*Thessalonica*	Salonika
Brundisium	Brindisi	*Leptis Magna*	(Libya)	*Theveste*	Tebessa
Burdigala	Bordeaux	*Londinium*	London	*Trapezus*	Trabzon
Byzantium	Byzantium	*Lugdunum*	Lyon	*Troesmis*	(Dobruja)
Caesaraugusta	Saragossa	*Mogontiacum*	Mainz	*Vindobona*	Vienna
Caesarea	Cherchell	*Mediolanum*	Milan		
Caesarodunum	Tours	*Melitene*	Malatya		
		Naissus	Niš		

FIGURE 68.

Hebros River valley. From there it turned inland toward *Hadrianopolis* (Edirne) before finally reaching Byzantium on the banks of the Bosphorus. When Byzantium became Constantinople in A.D. 330, one could say that a single artery made up of two segments, the Via Appia and the Via Aegnatia, directly linked the two capitals of the empire (FIGURE 71).

Thereafter it was the West's turn. After the province of Gallia Narbonensis was subdued around the turn of the second century B.C., the Via Domitia, built around 120 B.C. by Proconsul Gnaius Domitius Enobarbus, went from the Alps to the Pyrenees, starting at Monginevro (terminus of the Via Fulvia) and heading down toward *Arelate* (Arles), *Nemausus* (Nîmes), and *Narbo Martius* (Narbonne). Arles and Nîmes were also linked with the "continuation" of the Via Iulia Augusta, which came all the way from the Italian border, passing through *Antipolis* (modern Antibes), *Forum Iulii* (Fréjus), *Aquae Sextiae* (Aix-en-Provence), and *Glanum* (St.-Rémy) (FIGURE 72).

FIGURE 69.
Reconstruction of the *miliarium aureum* (golden milestone). Engraving from the *Voyage pittoresque* of the Abbé de Saint Non.

FIGURE 70.
Rome, Roman Forum. Fragment of the marble base of the *miliarium aureum*.

FIGURE 71, OPPOSITE
The Via Aegnatia near Philippi, Greece.

FIGURE 72.
Roman road at
Ambrussum, in the
Hérault (France).

In the Iberian Peninsula, according to Strabo, Rome had built more than
two thousand miles of roads by the time Augustus died in A.D. 14. This total
was later to reach almost seven thousand. A coastal route—the continuation
of the Via Domitia first called *Via Maxima*, then *Via Augusta*—went from
the Pyrenees to *Carthago Nova* (modern Cartagena), passing through *Barcino*
(Barcelona), *Tarraco* (Tarragona) (FIGURE 73), *Saguntum* (Sagunto), and
Valentia (Valencia). Starting at Cartagena, another road cut through the inte-
rior, passing through *Corduba* (Cordoba) and reached as far as *Gades* (modern
Cádiz) and the Atlantic Ocean. The entire route, as registered on the milestones, which used the Atlantic (*ad oceanum*) as their reference point, totaled
980 miles, equal to about 1,500 kilometers. At *Dertosa* (Tortosa), another
road branched off from the coastal route. Ranging up the Ebro River valley,
it went all the way to the northwestern extremity of the peninsula, to
Brigantium (La Coruña), passing through the mining region of Asturias.

FIGURE 73.
Roman honorary
arch at Berà, near
Tarragona (Spain).
First–second
century A.D.

FIGURE 74.
One of the four silver
"goblets of Vicarello"
(Lago di Bracciano,
Italy), with the route
from Cádiz to Rome,
including the main
cities and relative
distances, inscribed
on the surface. They
were probably votive
offerings made by a
traveler at the nearby
Santuario di Apollo
(*Aquae Apollinares*).
Late first century B.C.
Rome, Museo
Nazionale Romano.

From here, starting at *Asturica Augusta* (Astorga), the *Via Argentea* ("silver
road") ran southward, also to Cádiz, passing through *Salmantica* (Salamanca),
Emerita Augusta (Mérida), *Italica*, and *Hispalis* (Seville) (FIGURES 74–75)
along the way. Another long road was the transverse route built by Vespasian,
which ran from Mérida to *Caesaraugusta* (Saragossa), passing through
Caesarobriga (Talavera), *Toletum* (Toledo), *Complutum* (Alcalà de Henares),
and *Segontia* (Sigüenza).

In Gaulish lands the road system, which was linked and integrated with
numerous important river routes, underwent its first major overhaul after

Augustus's journey there in 27 B.C. Agrippa undertook the project during the years he was governor of the provinces conquered by Caesar. Foremost among these roads was the one that, according to Strabo, was the shortest, most well-traveled route from Italy, the "road of the Gauls" par excellence. It started with the Via Domitia at Monginevro and, following the upper Rhône valley, went to *Lugdunum* (Lyon), "capital" of Celtic Gaul and its main road hub. Two important roads started at Lyon: one running southward along the Rhône to Arles (with a branch running eastward to *Massalia*, modern-day Marseilles), the other cutting across Aquitaine through the Garonne valley to

FIGURE 75. Inscription.

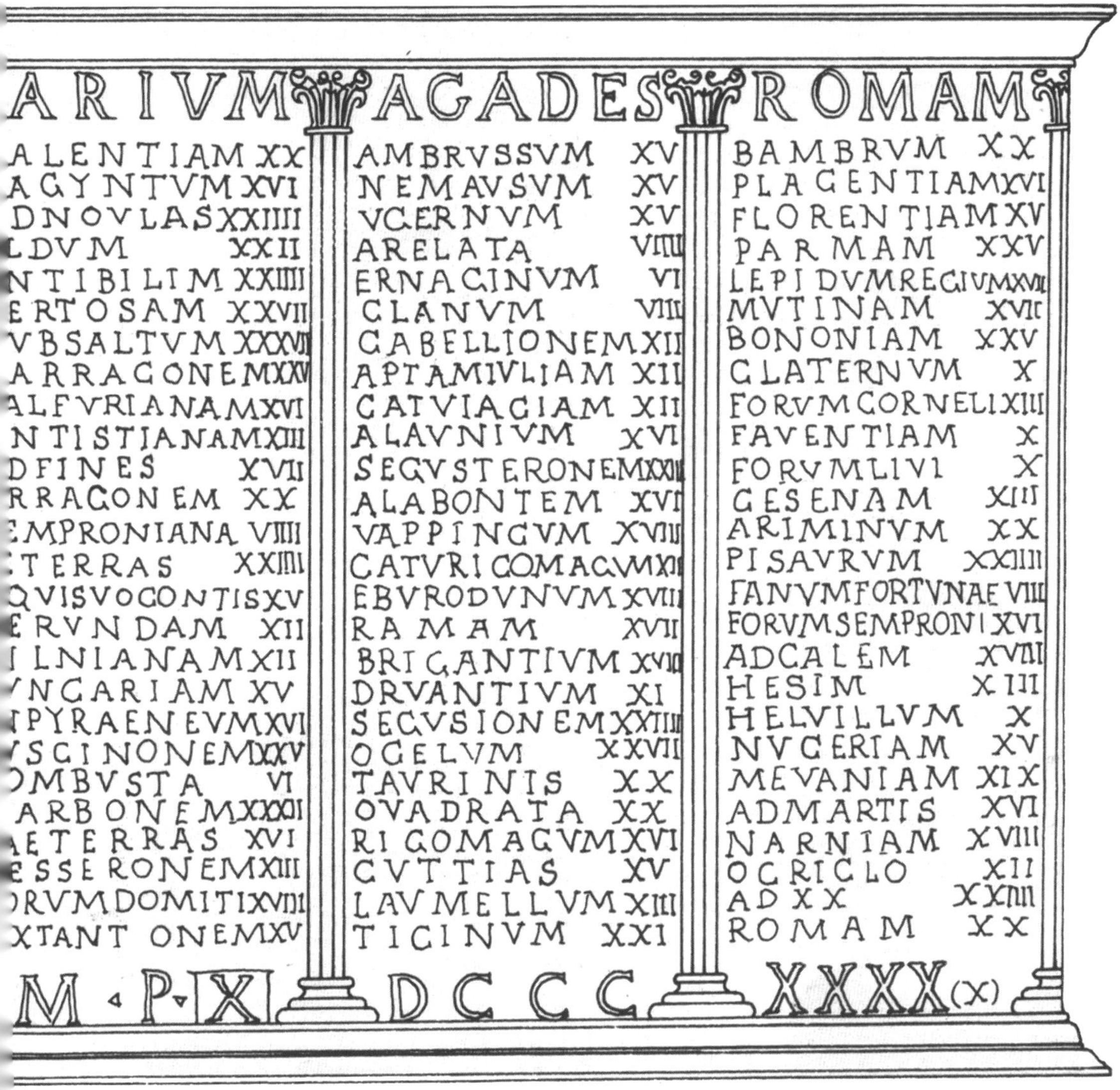

ARIVM · AGADES · ROMAM

ALENTIAM XX	AMBRVSSVM XV	BAMBRVM XX
AGYNTVM XVI	NEMAVSVM XV	PLAGENTIAM XVI
DNOVLAS XXIIII	VGERNVM XV	FLORENTIAM XV
LDVM XXII	ARELATA VIII	PARMAM XXV
NTIBILIM XXIIII	ERNAGINVM VI	LEPIDVMREGIVM XVII
ERTOSAM XXVII	GLANVM VIII	MVTINAM XVII
VBSALTVM XXXVI	GABELLIONEM XII	BONONIAM XXV
ARRAGONEM XXV	APTAMIVLIAM XII	GLATERNVM X
ALFVRIANAM XVI	CATVIAGIAM XII	FORVMGORNELI XIII
NTISTIANAM XIII	ALAVNIVM XVI	FAVENTIAM X
DFINES XVII	SEGVSTERONEM XXII	FORVMLIVI X
RRAGONEM XX	ALABONTEM XVI	GESENAM XIII
EMPRONIANA VIIII	VAPPINGVM XVIII	ARIMINVM XX
TERRAS XXIIII	CATVRIGOMAGVM XXI	PISAVRVM XXIIII
QVISVOGONTIS XV	EBVRODVNVM XVIII	FANVMFORTVNAE VIII
ERVNDAM XII	RAMAM XVII	FORVMSEMPRONI XVI
ILNIANAM XII	BRIGANTIVM XVII	ADCALEM XVIII
NGARIAM XV	DRVANTIVM XI	HESIM XIII
PYRAENEVM XVI	SEGVSIONEM XXIIII	HELVILLVM X
SCINONEM XXV	OGELVM XXVII	NVGERIAM XV
OMBVSTA VI	TAVRINIS XX	MEVANIAM XIX
ARBONEM XXXI	OVADRATA XX	ADMARTIS XVI
ETERRAS XVI	RIGOMAGVM XVI	NARNIAM XVIII
ESSERONEM XIII	GVTTIAS XV	OGRICLO XII
RVMDOMITI XVIII	LAVMELLVM XIII	AD XX XXIIII
XTANTONEM XV	TICINVM XXI	ROMAM XX

M ◁ P▾ X | D C C C | XXXX (X)

91

Burdigala (Bordeaux), where it was joined by another road coming from Narbonne by way of Toulouse. Continuing the Rhone route was another important road that headed north, dividing into several different branches at *Durocortorum* (Reims). The main branch continued on to *Gesoriacum*, later renamed *Bononia* (Boulogne), on the English Channel, from whence one crossed over into Britannia at the port of *Dubrae* (Dover).

In Britannia the main road axis ran north-south, starting at *Londinium* (London), passing through *Lindum* (Lincoln), and ending at *Eburacum* (York). The extension of this road went as far as the defense works built along the border with Scotland: Hadrian's Wall and that of Antoninus Pius. For a while, this constituted the northernmost point ever reached by a Roman road (FIGURE 76). The two most important transverse routes also branched out from London: to the southwest as far as *Durnovaria* (modern Dorchester) and *Isca* (Exeter) by way of *Calleva* (Silchester); and toward Wales by way of *Verulamium* (St. Albans) and ending at *Deva* (Chester).

Back in Gaul, two roads of strategic importance also set out from Durocortorum on their way to the banks of the Rhine, which the first of these reached at *Colonia Agrippina* (Cologne), the second at Mainz, after passing through *Augusta Treverorum* (Trier). A vital link was thus established with the road system of the *limes*, the fortified boundary line established along the long road that flanked the great river's right bank all the way to its mouth. This "Rhine road," for all intents and purposes, began at the Splugen Pass in the Alps. After reaching the river almost immediately at *Curia* (Chur), the road followed it consistently through *Brigantium* (Bregenz) and past the southern shore of its lake, through *Vindonissa* (Windisch) and *Augusta Raurica* (modern Augst, near Basel). From here it continued on through *Argentorate* (Strasbourg), Mainz, *Confluentes* (Koblenz), *Rigomagus* (Remagen), *Bonna* (Bonn), Cologne, *Novaesium* (Neuss), *Vetera* (Xanthen), and *Triectum* (Utrecht), before arriving at *Lugdunum Batavorum* (Leyden) on the North Sea. It is worth remembering at this point the two great bridges that the Romans built over the Rhine: first the temporary wooden one that Caesar ordered built (in ten days) in 55 B.C. between Andernach and Koblenz; then the more stable one that Constantine had built in masonry 350 years later, a 420-meter span between Cologne and the "bridgehead" of *Divitia* (Deutz) that sprouted up on the right bank. (One peculiarity of the roads of Gaul was the use of the Celtic "league" [*leuga* or *lega*] as a unit of measurement, made official at the time of Septimius Severus. It was equal to 1.5 miles or 2.22 km.)

In the provinces of Rhaetia, Noricum, and Pannonia (corresponding roughly with present-day Switzerland, Bavaria, Austria, and Hungary), the main roads—variously interconnected among themselves—also originated in Alpine passes and then headed north or east toward the Danube, which constituted another of the long and important borders of the empire. One such road was a continuation of the Via Claudia. It started at the Brenner Pass, then went on to *Aeni Pons* (modern Innsbruck, whose German name is a

FIGURE 76.
A section of Hadrian's
Wall in Scotland.

literal translation of its Latin one, which means "bridge over the Inn river"), *Parthanus* (Partenkirchen), and *Augusta Vindelicorum* (Augsburg). Another, continuing the Via Iulia Augusta, started at the Monte Croce Carnico Pass and went to *Lauriacum* (Lorch), with an offshoot going to *Virunum* (Klagenfurt).

The Danube, for its part, was closely followed along the right bank by a road of its own that passed through *Castra Regina* (modern Ratisbon), *Vindobona* (Vienna), *Caruntum* (Petronell), and *Aquincum* (Budapest). The road of the Julian Alps also led to Budapest, passing through *Emona* (Ljubljana) and branching off into the two great Balkan arteries that passed through the Drava and Sava valleys and reached the Danube at *Sirmium* (Mitrovica) and *Singidunum* (Belgrade).

The "Danube road" proceeded through the province of *Moesia* (modern Bulgaria), passing through *Viminacium*, *Ratiaria*, and *Oescus* before reaching the great river's delta. And since it was connected to the "Rhine road," it could be said that a single road ran from the North Sea all the way to the Black Sea. Another aspect of the "Danube road" that should not pass without mention is that despite major destruction and alteration, it still contains documentary evidence of one of the most spectacular undertakings of Roman road building. At the so-called Iron Gates near *Turnu Severin* (ancient *Drobetae*) on the Serbian-Romanian border, one entire stretch of this road was cut directly into the rock more than three meters above the river, some eighty centimeters of it jutting out over the water, resting on powerful wooden trusses wedged inside long holes bored into the rock face. A commemorative inscription—the so-called *Tabula Traiani* ("Trajan's Tablet")— was carved into the rock; this marker has recently been raised some twenty meters to protect it from rising waters caused by dam building. Bearing the emperor's name, the tablet bears witness to this day of that exceptional feat of engineering. A few kilometers downstream, atop twenty gigantic stone pylons whose remains could still be seen at the bottom of the river in the mid-nineteenth century, there once stood the bridge built, also for Trajan, by Apollodorus of Damascus, crossing the Danube with its wooden spans. One can still see a representation of it on Trajan's Column in Rome. Over this bridge ran the road that linked Moesia to *Dacia* (modern Romania), extending as far as the Carpathian foothills (FIGURE 77).

Another important road on the Balkan Peninsula started at Sirmium and forked in two directions. One branch went to Byzantium by way of *Naissus* (modern Niš), *Serdica* (Sofia), and *Philippopolis* (Plovdiv). The other went to Salonika (where it intersected with the Via Aegnatia), after which it continued on through Thessaly and Boeotia as far as Corinth. Corinth was also a destination (and Athens another) of the long coastal road that began at Istria and continued down the coasts of Dalmatia and Epirus and around the Gulfs of Patras and Corinth.

FIGURE 77.
Model reconstruction
of Trajan's bridge over
the Danube. Rome,
Museo della Civiltà
Romana.

In the empire's Asian provinces, from the Anatolian peninsula to Syria (and for a while in Armenia and Mesopotamia as well), the Roman road network did little more than superimpose itself on the one created in its time by the Persian Empire and expanded by the Hellenistic rulers. There were, however, various improvements made on the basis of specific needs. On the one hand, there were strategic considerations concerning the frontier with the Parthian kingdom, which led to the construction or renovation of a number of roads in times of, or in anticipation of, war or military expeditions. One such was undertaken during Trajan's Parthian war by the Ninth "Hispanic" legion, which set out from *Emesa*—modern Homs—in Syria and pushed on to the Euphrates. On the other hand, there were the needs dictated by sea outlets of caravan routes from Mesopotamia and the Syrian and Arabian deserts, which originated in the Middle and Far East. One great road, which retraced the ancient "Royal Road" of the Persians and started at Susa, crossed the entire Anatolian peninsula, passing through *Ancyra* (Ankara)—where one link road went on to Sinope on the Black Sea and another went to Byzantium on the Bosphorus—and finally arrived at Ephesus on the Aegean. And through Ephesus also passed the coastal road on its way from Pergamon and Smyrna, before continuing on to Halicarnassos, Attalia, and Tarsus and ending up at Antioch. Another coastal route ran along the shores of the Black Sea as far as *Trapezus* (Trabzon) (FIGURE 78).

FIGURE 78.
Remains of road pave-
ment in the city
of Petra (Jordan).

In Syria and Arabia, the caravan cities of Palmyra, Apamea, Damascus, and Petra were genuine road hubs, while the most important point of convergence was the great port city of Antioch. At Antioch another important coastal route originated, linking Asia and Africa; it ran as far as *Pelusium* (near the modern Port Said) in the Nile delta after passing through the Phoenician gates of Sidon and Tyre, *Caesarea* (FIGURE 79) and Gaza in Palestine, and the Sinai Peninsula.

FIGURE 79.
Road in the urban
center of the ancient
town of Caesarea
(Israel).

In Egypt, in addition to the very ancient road that went up the left bank
of the Nile, routes that led to Red Sea ports such as *Myus Hormus* became
very important, serving as termini for caravans from the Arabian peninsula,
Ethiopia, and the Horn of Africa. One such road was the *Via Nova Hadriani*,
which began at *Antinoupolis*. At Alexandria began yet another great coastal
road that covered the entire shore of North Africa, passing through
Cyrenaica, *Africa Proconsularis*, Numidia, and Mauritania before arriving at

FIGURE 80.
Leptis Magna, Libya.
Street with benches.

FIGURE 80.
Leptis Magna, Libya.
Street with benches.

Tingis (Tangiers) and *Sala* (Rabat) in Morocco. Along the way it stopped at
Cyrene, *Leptis Magna* (FIGURE 80), *Oea* (modern Tripoli), Sabratha, *Tacapae*
(Gabès), *Hadrumetum* (Sousse), Carthage, *Hippo Regius*, and *Iol Caesarea*
(modern Cherchell). This vital artery, especially its central section, was a terminal point for the caravan routes that, as one reads on a milestone from

FIGURE 81.
Leptis Magna, Libya.
Milestone of the road
that went from the coast
to the inland desert
("*in mediterraneo*").

Leptis Magna (FIGURE 81), went off "*in mediterraneo*," that is, into the
Libyan hinterland, to places like *Cydamus* (the oasis of Ghadames), the
destination of Saharan trails originating in equatorial Africa. A dense web
of local roads, moreover, covered the densely urbanized territories of
Proconsular Africa (Tunisia) and *Mauretania Caesariensis* (east-central

FIGURE 82.
The gate of the city
of Tiddis (Algeria).

Algeria) (FIGURE 82). Radiating outward mostly from Carthage, this network joined up with the system of military roads serving the defensive require-ments of the *Fossatum Africae*, the fortified line around the Chotts and the sub-Saharan oases, which also served as a terminus for various caravan routes originating from points south.

Naturally, the African coastal road linked up, through the Strait of Gibraltar, with the Via Augusta in Spain, thus closing the great ring of roads laid down by Rome around the *Mare Nostrum*.

Built for the purpose of creating the maximum ease of communication between the center and periphery of the empire, all the great Roman roads were equipped to allow a state "postal service" (*cursus publicus*) to function with the greatest possible efficiency. Already in operation during the republi-can era, the *cursus publicus* was institutionalized and reorganized by Augustus. As Suetonius tells us (*Aug.* XLIX, 5), the emperor "first placed young men, then vehicles, at specific intervals along the military roads . . . so that what

FIGURE 83.
Stela of a soldier in
the Imperial Guard
on horseback (*eques
singularis*). Rome,
Museo della Civiltà
Romana. Copy of the
original in the Vatican
Museums, Rome.

was happening in each of the
provinces could be divulged and
known as quickly and easily as possible." The historian adds: "This
seemed the most practical solution,
so that those bearing the messages
directly from any location could be
questioned on any subject, if circumstances dictated."

At first, "public" slaves, soldiers,
or young men stationed in the cities
along the route performed this service. They were later replaced by a
regular corps of couriers on horseback (the *tabellarii*)—supplemented

FIGURE 84.
Valle di Baccano, near
Rome. Excavation of
the *mansio* of *Baccanae*
along the ancient
Via Cassia.

when necessary by "postal carts"—working in relay shifts. They would replace one another for very long stretches, with frequent changes of horses at assigned "change posts" called *mutationes*, positioned at intervals ranging between seven and twelve miles apart (10 and 18 km). At a rate of five miles (7.4 km) per hour, one day's travel covered about fifty miles (roughly 75 km), and a dispatch rider sent from Rome to Brindisi along the Via Appia would arrive in seven or eight days (FIGURE 83).

The real "rest stops" outfitted for extended stays and for spending the night were the *mansiones* (FIGURE 84), usually situated one day's journey apart and equipped with every sort of service and provisions for men, horses, and vehicles. They had inns, stables, and carriage houses, workshops and specialized personnel working under a *praepositus*: stable hands, blacksmiths,

carpenters (*carpentarii*, from the name of the most commonly used traveling carriages, the *carpentum*), veterinarians, coachmen, and administrators. Often there was a "station" or guardpost for the "road police," whose officers were called *stationarii*. Thieves, troublemakers, and brigands were some the most common users of the roads, and their ambushes and attacks were a source of constant danger to travelers.

Alongside the public structures reserved for the couriers and for those who traveled in any capacity for the state, there were also private establishments that offered wayfarers common meals and food supplies, baths, lodging, and shelter for animals. On the whole, the public structures and private concerns allowed people to make the most of the great roads, especially as to rapidity

of movement. Aside from the couriers of the *cursus publicus*, the average daily distance covered by a "normal" traveler was probably around thirty miles (slightly under 45 km). But on foot, with a beast of burden, one couldn't travel more than fifteen to twenty miles a day (maximum 30 km). As for soldiers, who moved quite rapidly on foot from one end of the empire to another, their normal daily traveling distance ranged between twenty and twenty-four miles (30 to 35 km), with one day of rest for every four days of marching (FIGURE 85).

FIGURE 85.
Relief of a transport carriage.

We also have documentation of exceptional feats of travel, however. Ovid remembers a private letter arriving in Rome from Brindisi after only nine days, averaging slightly over forty miles (59 km) per day. Cicero, for his part, used to get letters in Naples from Rome in only four or five days. Cicero also speaks (*pro Roscio*, VII, 19) of traveling from Rome to *Ameria*, in Umbria, at night, in a fast carriage, covering a distance of fifty-six miles (83 km) in ten hours, an average of five and a half miles an hour (FIGURE 86). According to Plutarch (*Cato maior*, 14, 4), in 191 B.C., Cato the censor made the journey from Brindisi to Rome in five days, averaging seventy-three miles (108 km) a day. Caesar achieved the same average in 46 B.C., according to Suetonious (*Caes.* LVI), when he traveled from Cordoba, Spain, to Rome on horseback for twenty-three consecutive days! But in 58 B.C. Caesar had done even better, managing to cover, also on horseback, a distance of eight hundred miles (1,182 km), from Rome to Lake Geneva, in only eight days, averaging a hundred miles (148 km) a day!

FIGURE 86.
Relief of a traveling carriage (a *raeda* or, more likely, a *carruca dormitoria*). Rome, Museo della Civiltà Romana. Copy of original in the Church of Maria Saal, near Klagenfurt (Austria).

The Most Durable of Monuments

Called the "longest monument" of the Roman world, the road system is also its most widespread monument, the one that left behind the greatest number of testimonies to itself. And this is also because it was the most composite: that is, formed by so many different elements.

First of all, there is the road itself, obviously, with its specific constants being the straight line, the raised roadway, and consistency of elevation. The straight line—that is, the straightaway—resulted from the priority given to reaching the "terminus" (and therefore the links and connections with medium-sized centers not on the main line) as quickly as possible. The raised roadway—its use of embankments (*aggeres*) to elevate the surface above the surrounding terrain—was dictated by safety considerations: Dangers presented by men could be better controlled with good visibility from above, and the dangers from natural phenomena (heavy rain, snowfalls, flooding, etc.) could be ameliorated. These same safety considerations also made it necessary to maintain a consistency of elevation—a "maintenance of height"—which meant avoiding as much as possible low-lying terrain, valley floors, and hollows, and instead favoring ridges (or watersheds) and hillsides.

As for the road surface, there were various different solutions, depending on need, feasibility, time, and place—even along different stretches of one same road, since the routes were usually very long. On the whole, the operative principle was that the road should last as long as possible with a minimum of maintenance and very rare instances of repair and renovation. This implied giving especial care to the roads' "foundations," which were adapted in accordance with a timely understanding of the nature of the ground. And the solutions for the surface varied as well. The commonest and simplest one consisted of leaving the natural earthen base, eventually beaten down, as the roadway: These were the *viae terrenae*, which could also be "cut" into the bedrock and then planed and smoothed as needed (and possibly also provided with horizontal grooves to prevent cart wheels from sliding and to give animals' hooves and people's shoes better purchase). One very common solution was to "pave" the surface with crushed stone or gravel; such roads were the *viae glareatae* (from *glarea* for gravel). The best solution, and also the most exacting, was to cover the road surface with large paving stones, unevenly polygonal in shape but perfectly imbedded and interconnected (aided, when necessary, by smaller stones used as wedges), smoothed on the surface and roughly "beveled" below. This is the method that gave us the *viae stratae* (or *viae lapidibus stratae*), that is, "paved roads" (or "roads paved with stones"), the word *stratae* being the past participle of the verb *sternere* ("to spread out or spread over"), used here as an adjective (FIGURE 87). It goes without saying that in the collective imagination this sort of road was and remains the Roman road par excellence—whether the paving stones, in keeping with what was locally available, were made of basaltic lava, commonly called *silex* ("hard stone" or "flint"), or white calcareous stone, granite, or in some cases sandstone or even tufa.

A "paved" road (and to a considerably lesser extent, a gravel road) required a special foundation that was usually created in successive layers inside a "trench" dug into the ground for this purpose. The "deep" layer (between 30 and 60 cm in depth) that formed the roadbed, was made up of large chips of hard stone (*statumen*) and topped, when necessary, by another layer (*rudus* or *ruderatio*) between twenty-five and thirty-nine centimeters thick, consisting of smaller rocks packed solidly together and held firm with lime and pozzolana (volcanic dust). Next came an "elastic" middle layer (*nucleus*) made up of sand and crushed stone (or gravel and shards of earthenware and plaster), which was then leveled by pounding or using heavy rollers. Finally, there was the outer revetment called the *pavimentum* (or *dorsus summum* or *summa crusta*), made up of stone slabs laid into a bed of sand.

The performance of the various operations required for the opening of a road is succinctly laid out by the poet Statius in a composition celebrating the construction of the Via Domitiana (*Silvae*, IV, 3, 40–55): "The first task was to design the furrows, eliminating all obstructions, and to dig a deep ditch in the ground. Then to fill the ditch variously and prepare the roadbed so as to prevent the ground from giving way and avoid having an unsteady foundation vacillate under the stones lain on top. Then one sees to tightening the road surface on both sides with blocks of stone and holding it in place with numerous curbstones. How many teams working at once! Some cut down trees and excavate stones from the hills; others smooth the blocks and plane the wood beams with irons. Some lay the stones side by side and complete the fabric with lime and pozzolana; others with great effort drain marshes and divert the courses of small streams!" (FIGURE 88).

Of course, the patterns could vary depending on specific local conditions, especially as regards the foundations. This is borne out, for example, by a stretch of road near Rochester in Britannia, where the customary apparatus of the roadbed rested on oak pilings driven deep into the marshy ground; or by a road on the unstable ground of the Hautes

FIGURE 87. Archaeological site of *Ferentum*, near Viterbo. A tract of the Via Ferentiensis as *decumanus* of the city.

FIGURE 88.
Construction of
a Roman road.

Fagnes area in Belgium (FIGURE 89), where the "sub-foundation" was created not only with pilings, but also with a superimposed weave of horizontal and vertical wood beams, while the outer revetment was made up of a kind of double pavement, with one layer of calcareous slabs bound together with clay and another layer of pebbles and gravel laid on top.

Whatever the type of paving used, the top surface of the roadway was normally curved or slightly pitched to allow rainwater to flow toward the drainage ditches on the sides and to prevent it from stagnating. The roadway was enclosed and held together on both sides by a "cordon" of stones (*umbones*) planted vertically into the ground and fitted, usually every three "steps" (3 m), with curbstones (*gomphi*) consisting of roughly cone-shaped stones. These curbstones could help one mount or dismount a horse and guide wayfarers in conditions of heavy snow or sandstorms (which would seem to explain their systematic presence along the roads in Gaul and North Africa). Finally, the road was flanked by sidewalks (*margines* or *crepidines*) whose breadth varied but was at least three meters, and whose surface was usually beaten earth or crushed stone and pebbles. Often at the sides of the paved roads, used by carts and carriages, were footpaths of beaten earth reserved for travelers on foot or on horseback.

As for the width of the roadway, by and large it was broad enough to allow two carts to overtake or pass each other. Measurements would vary, even on the same road; indeed, the longer it was and the more territories it covered, the more varied in size it would be. The ancient law of the "Twelve Tables" from the mid-fifth century B.C. established a minimum width of eight feet (2.3 m) for straightaways and sixteen feet (4.73 m) for curves. As time went on, the median width of the great roads rose to between fourteen and twenty feet (4 to 6 m). Given the peculiarities of the means of transport, the roads could allow for considerable sloping (but not more than 20 percent) and a rather modest bend radius between five and eight meters.

Strict respect for the established guidelines of road building made it frequently (and onerously) necessary to confront and resolve problems of every sort by creating many demanding "works of art." With their proverbial sense of practicality, the Romans did everything possible to avoid problems, but did not shrink from confronting them when it proved inevitable. They preferred that their roads be on accessible, solid, and level ground, and even be pleasant to look upon, at a height that could be reached without too much effort, and they always kept an eye out for natural springs, water wells, and places suitable for rest and refreshment along the way. But they

FIGURE 89.
The various phases of Roman road construction in the marshy area of Hautes-Fagnes in Belgium, with wooden roadbed substrate.

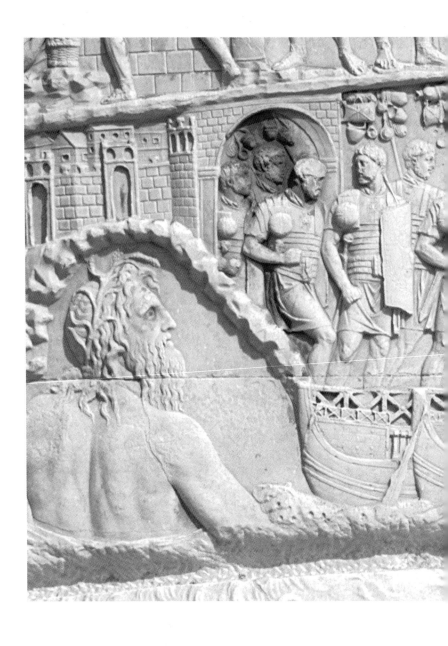

FIGURE 90.
Trajan's pontoon
bridge over the
Danube, in the
reliefs on Trajan's
Column, Rome.

were not afraid to tackle impassable and difficult areas, marshes and deserts, mountain passes and lowlands, hindrances and unforeseen events, and they managed to overcome these impediments every time with the appropriate adjustments.

Foremost among the necessary, unavoidable "works of art" they made were, of course, the bridges—which, moreover, being still quite numerous and often very well preserved and able to support an undoubtedly "heavier" form of traffic, remain the most important testimonies to the roads them-

selves. Aside from those made of wood (and sometimes even pontoons)
(FIGURE 90), the type of bridge of which the Romans proved themselves
masters was made of one or more arches resting on pillars or piers (*pilae*).
These supports were erected as far as possible outside the river bed or at the
most favorable points without regard for irregularities in the spans (as a
result, the arches are not always equal in breadth); they were built for the
most part according to the technique of *opus quadrata* or "square work,"
out of parallelepiped blocks of stone, more rarely out of cement with brick

FIGURE 91.
The Alcantara bridge
over the Tagus, near
the border between
Spain and Portugal.

facing (FIGURE 91). They were almost always quite massive. This bulk not only limited the aperture of the archways but presented a danger from the force of the water in times of flood; for this reason it was necessary to open up large "windows" or subsidiary arches at a height greater than the high-water level in normal times. The arches, either semicircular or slightly depressed, were built by aligning radially hewn stones set in place on top of a wooden centerpiece or frame. They were usually set high above the water,

FIGURE 92.
The ruins of the
Augustan bridge of the
Via Flamina, over the
Nera River near Narni.

often in excess of thirty meters, a height often reached and surpassed by the apertures of the arches alone; such was the case of the great span, now collapsed, of the Augustan bridge of the Via Flaminia over the Nera River in Narni, Umbria, which was thirty-two meters high (FIGURE 92).

Being generally of considerable height to avoid the dangers of rising flood-waters, the bridges were usually "donkey-backed," that is, with the roadway

FIGURE 93.
Pont St.-Martin
(Valle d'Aosta, Italy).
Roman bridge over
the Lys torrent, con-
sisting of one single
span over thirty meters
wide. Late second
century B.C.

inclined both on the ascent and
descent (FIGURES 93–94). As for
the width, it conformed to that of
the road, but was usually around
four or five meters. The length normally depended on the breadth of
the river bed to be spanned, and it
was increased by multiplying the
arches. The longest bridge built by
the Romans, previously mentioned,
was the one that used wooden arches
to span the Danube near Turnu
Severin in Romania, which measured 1127 meters.

Aside from the bridges, there
were also viaducts, built variously to
avoid tiresome inclines, to maintain
a consistent road level through
craggy terrain, or to incline the road
gradually toward an approaching

FIGURE 94.
Villeneuve (Valle
d'Aosta, Italy).
Roman bridge,
first century B.C.

FIGURE 95.
Aymaville (Valle d'Aosta,
Italy). "Pondel" bridge,
over the Val di Cogne
torrent, 50 meters long
and 55 meters high. It
has two superimposed
passageways, the top one
uncovered and the bot-
tom one covered. Third
century B.C.

Veduta della magnifica Sostruzione fabricata per reggere la falda del Monte, e per render la Via Appia più commoda, e meno declive tra la valle, e le opposte Colline Appio Claudio il Censore l'anno 442 di Roma intraprese la Via dalla Porta Capena sin'alla Città di Capua. L'Architettura di quest'Opera si rende particolare nella costruzione degli Archi, per esser quelli antica maniera usata prima de'tempi de'Cesari. Quest'opera è fabricata a corsi di pietre quadrate lunghe di Pietra Albana. La detta Strada è fabricata di grandi lastre di Selci ben connesse. Questo Edificio era prima mol-to elevato dal piano antico, ora ricoperto dalle rovine, e si vede lungo ... da Albano un miglio in circa.

rise. These consisted either of a succession of arches or of gigantic embankments supported on either side by powerful walls made according to the
technique of "polygonal work" and more often "square work," using immense
squared blocks of stone arranged in rows. The walls could be externally reinforced with spurs or buttresses. Transverse partitions served to link the outer
stone revetments, between which was packed the mixture of dirt and stones
that constituted the main body of the structure. At the base of the viaduct,
there might be small, open arches allowing ditches, or perhaps people and
animals, to pass underneath. A fine example among the surviving viaducts is
that found along the Via Appia near Ariccia, dating from the second century
B.C. (with later restorations and alterations), which runs for slightly more
than 230 meters at a maximum height of about 13 meters (FIGURES 96–98).

Among the "works of art" strictly linked to the nature of the terrain, perhaps the most frequent were those created to bring the road plane to a level
different from that of the surrounding countryside. These were trenches (or
"cuts") and embankments (or "mounds"), often used simultaneously when
the roadway had to be brought first down, by means of excavation, then up,
by means of embankments or causeways, or vice versa. Both adjustments created artificial escarpments and thus almost always involved the construction
of additional protective structures, such as support walls to maintain the

FIGURES 96–97,
OPPOSITE
The Via Appia
viaduct, in the
Ariccia valley.

FIGURE 98, ABOVE
The Ariccia viaduct
in a print by Piranesi.

embankment at the height of
the road level or "counterscarps" or
retaining walls to support the sides
of the trench. Surviving testimony
show us that the Romans could
handle even deep "cuts" with
considerable skill, as in the case
of the so-called "Broken Mountain"
(Montagna Spaccata) in the hills
between Cumae and Pozzuoli in
Campania, where a deep wedge-
shaped trench with stone walls
revetted in *opus reticulatum* ("reticu-
lar work") allowed the Via Campana
to pass through. (It is still used
by modern roads.) Another such
case is the nearby *Arcus Felix* (Happy
Arch) (FIGURE 99) serving the
Via Domitiana, where the cut is
"revetted" with a powerful barrel-
vault surmounted by arches forming
a viaduct at the summit of the
"trench."

In a similar class to the "cuts" are
the operations performed to remove
rocky spurs or to cut away the rock
face on slopes in mountainous areas.
A famous example of the former
is the cut of the Pesco Montano at
Terracina, executed with extreme
precision and regularity over a height
of roughly thirty-eight meters to
open a passage to the Via Appia.
An example of the latter case is the
220-meter stretch of "Alpine road"
near Donnaz in the Valle d'Aosta,
where the roadway (including a
milestone) is cut directly into the
solid rock, almost five meters wide
(FIGURE 100).

Tunnels, on the other hand—
passages excavated blindly into
the earth—were truly exceptional
undertakings. But they were a last
resort used only when there was

FIGURE 99.
Viaduct of the Via
Domitiana, known
as the Arco Felice, in
the Campania region
of Italy.

FIGURE 100.
Donnaz (Valle
d'Aosta, Italy). The
"Road of the Gauls"
cut out of the rock.

no other solution or when they were the most convenient, and drastic, solution to a fundamental problem of passage. This was the case with the Furlo tunnel near Fossombrone in the Marches, which allowed the Via Flaminia to overcome an obstacle that would otherwise have forced it to take a long and roundabout mountain route (FIGURE 101). The tunnel was excavated at the behest of the emperor Vespasian in 77–76 B.C. (as stated in the commemorative inscription carved into the rock face over one of the entrances) at the narrowest point of the Condigliano River gorge; it measures just under 40 meters in length, 6 meters in height, and at least 5.47 meters wide. Right next to it, however, is another, smaller and much older tunnel (dating from 220 B.C.) that is 8 meters long, 3.30 meters wide, and 4.45 meters high. It should be added that the present-day Via Flaminia, direct heir to the ancient one, still passes through Vespasian's tunnel!

On the subject of tunnels, one of the few names of Roman road engineers that we know—that of Lucius Cocceius Auctus—was handed down to us by Strabo, who mentions him as the author of the so-called *Crypta* of Cocceius, a tunnel running under the Monte Grillo in the Phlegrean Fields area near Naples, connecting the Lake of Avernus with Cumae. It was almost one kilometer long and perfectly rectilinear, with an average width and height of 4.5 to 5 meters, with vertical and oblique apertures as

much as 30 meters high. Other
works that can be attributed to the
same engineer are the "extension"
of the same tunnel under the Monte
di Cuma, as well as the *Crypta
Neapolitana*, serving the coastal road
between Naples and Pozzuoli and
running under the hills that descend
from the Vomero to Posillipo.

Finally, it must be said that the
longest and most widespread monument of the Roman world was also
the most durable: not only and not
so much because of the countless
surviving archaeological specimens,
but above all because of the service
they have continued to provide since
the end of antiquity. In spite of
neglect and destruction, the Roman
road network, as a whole—and
especially for Western Europe—
has served as the foundation of the
entire modern road system up to the
present day, that is, up to the advent
of the superhighway. In Algeria, the
road cut into the rock and leading
out of the Aures mountains (the
ancient *Arausio Mons*), through the
Tighanimine gorges and toward the
desert, is still the same—except for
the asphalt, added by the French—
as when the Romans opened it in
145 A.D. On the smooth rock face
of the high ridge into which the
road was cut, one can still read
the commemorative inscription
carved by the legionaries who had
come from Syria to quell a revolt
among the natives and ended up
being enlisted to undertake this
project: "Under the Emperor Caesar
Titus Aelius Adrianus Antoninus
Augustus Pius, father of the country,
consul for the second time, the

FIGURE 101.
The Furlo tunnel
allowing the Via
Flaminia to pass
through. Near
Fossombrone, Marches
region of Italy.

125

detachment of the Sixth Armored Legion, on the orders of Prastina Messalinus, Imperial Legate and Propraetor, built this road."

As for the superhighways, we cannot help but notice that they have drawn inspiration from the same principles and the same criteria of construction (and have often retraced the same routes) as the great Roman roads. One need only cite by way of example the Autostrada del Sole ("Highway of the Sun"), which in its long segment between Bologna and Piacenza follows the ancient Via Aemilia, running parallel and adjacent to it. The railroads had already done the same, as demonstrated, for example, by the *direttissima* ("direct line") between Rome and Formia, which for the most part follows the route of the Via Appia. All of which proves that the route choices made by the Roman engineers were the right ones, that is, the ones dictated by nature, and that among their many merits should also be mentioned the ability to find and exploit these routes.

The longevity of Rome's roads owes much to the countless and sometimes unlikely linguistic vestiges, starting with the very words used in the Western languages (the Romance, Germanic, and English tongues) to designate the concept of "road" or "street." While the classical term *via* (with all its derivatives) has survived unaltered only in Italian (though it appears sometimes in Spanish and Portuguese, and in the French word *voie* as well), the Roman word *strata*, used to designate a paved road (*via strata*), reappears in the English *street*, in the German *strasse*, and the Italian *strada*. From the Latin adjective *rupta*, on the other hand (meaning "broken" or "interrupted"), which in the Middle Ages was used to designate an old Roman road in disrepair, come the French *route* (like the Portuguese *ruta*) and the English *road*. But there's more: the French *rue* and the Portuguese *rua* come from the Late Latin (and Italian) word *ruga*, which is still used in Venice, along with its diminutive *rugheta*, to designate a city street lined with shops; the Spanish (and Venetian) *calle* come from the Latin *callis* (path or trail), while the Latin noun *vicus*, designating an urban street, survives in the Italian *vico* and *vicolo*. But that's not all: from the Latin *calciata*, used in the expression *via caliciata* to designate a road paved with calcareous stone, are derived the Spanish *calzada* and the French *chaussé*; while the French *carrouge* and the Catalan *carrer* (as well as the Genoese-dialect *carruggio*) come from the Latin *quadrivium* ("crossroads") through its popular corruption as *quadruvium*.

In Italy there are terms and expressions, varying from region to region, used to designate those stretches of Roman roads that still survive in one form or another along their original routes, though long "declassé" and sometimes reduced to mere trails or entirely abandoned: these range from *via romana* or *romea* ("Roman road" or "Romish road") to *via petrata* ("stone road"), *via silicata* ("silicate road"), or *via calcata* ("trampled road"), to *via persa* ("lost road") and even *stradazza* ("nasty road"). The term *selciatella* (diminutive of *selciato*, "pavement"—from *silex*), on the other hand, has become a place name, and the list of similarly derived place names is practically endless. Just within the confines of Italy, there are numerous cities that have their origins in way stations where people stopped to rest, to meet, and to engage in commerce, which were planned from the moment the great roads were first built and are usually situated more or less at the halfway point. The names of such cities usually contained the term *forum* followed by an appellation derived, like the name of the road, from the name of the "builder." They continue to be called by their ancient names, in "revised" but usually transparent forms. For example, Forlì was originally *Forum Livii*; Forlimpopoli, *Forum Popilii*; Fossombrone, *Forum Sempronii*; Fordongianus, *Forum Traiani*; other minor instances include Fornovo, from *Forum Novum*, and also the French examples of Fréjus, from *Forum Iulii*, and the Fourvières hill outside of Lyon, derived from *Forum Vetus*. And from the name of one of the many *fora*, Forum Iulii (in the location of the modern city of Cividale), comes the name, by way of contraction, of the region of Friuli; while the Via Iulia (Augusta) gives its name to the Venezia Giulia region. But perhaps foremost among such Italian regions is Emilia, whose very name—the same name it bore in Roman times—derives from the ancient road that still runs through it.

There also are population centers that sprang up after the eclipse of the ancient world but whose names nevertheless derive from the Roman road along which they were formed. Among the many such towns are those originally called *Postumia* (and now called Postioma, Postaime, and Costuma) after the Via Postumia; as well as Agna, after the *Via Annia*; and Loreggio, after the Via Aurelia. Other town names, such as Stra and Stradella, refer more generically to the road. There are also countless place names derived from milestones—that is, which reflect the information once contained on the milestones. Examples of this phenomenon include the many villages called Quarto or Quinto or Tor di Quinto (from *ad quartum* or *ad quintum*—"at the fourth" or "fifth" milestone, the *miliarium* or *lapidem* being implied); Terzo or Valterzo (from *tertium*, "third") or, in France, Thiers; Ottavello, Tavello, or Tavo (from *ad octavum*); Annone and Castello d'Annone (from *ad nonum*, "at the ninth"); Pontedecimo (from *ad decimum*, "at the tenth"); Tricesimo (*ad tricesimum*, "at the thirteenth"); and so on.

Still other place names have their origins in specific situations related to the roads or to the "works of art" made for the roads, as the case of Trebbio, which comes from *Trivium* ("triple crossroad"); Codroipo, from *quadrivium* ("crossroad" of four roads); or Arzere and Cavarzere, which come from *agger*, the embankment under the "superelevated" roads, which are also behind such place names as La Levata, Ca' della Leva, Corte Levata, La Leva, and so on. The name of the Furlo tunnel is a modern form of the ancient *Forulus*; and the toponym Pietra Pertosa (echoed in the French *Pierre Pertuis*) implies "cut rock." And what of the French word for house, *maison*, which derives from the Latin *mansio*, meaning a post station along the road? The German *Brucke* (bridge), for its part, derives from the French expression *pont de briques*, or "brick bridge," which is precisely what the Roman bridges often were, compared to the wooden footbridges of the Germanic tribes. And while we're on the subject, the place name of Alcantara—which we encounter in Sicily, Spain, and North Africa and which derives from the Arabic *el-Kantara*, or "the bridge"—is always an indication of a Roman bridge in the area.

As a final observation, even the apparently innocent names of the Dutch cities of Utrecht and Maastricht derive directly from the Latin *traiectum*, "ferry" or "ferry crossing," as each of those cities, respectively, took shape at the point where the Rhine and the Meuse (*Maas*) were crossed by the ferry of an ancient Roman road.

BIBLIOGRAPHICAL NOTE

The scholarship on the roads of Rome is vast and continuously being enriched, especially as regards specific areas, individual roads and road designs, and local and regional road networks. What is missing, if anything—taking for granted, of course, the syntheses contained in encyclopedias and textbooks—is a truly comprehensive study treating the entire Roman road system in all its various aspects. There are, however, a number of good introductory and generalized works, some of recent date. The most important are:

V. Von Hagen, *The Roads that Led to Rome* (Cleveland and New York, 1967).

R. Chevalier, *Les voies romaines* (Paris, 1972), with 40 pages of bibliography, divided by subject, covering works up to the early 1970s.

G. Radke, *Viae Publicae Romane* (Ital. trans., Bologna, 1981).

J. P. Adam, "Le strade e le opere di ingegneria." In *L'arte di costruire presso i romani: Materiale e techniche* (Ital. trans., Milan, 1988).

Viae publicae romanae, exh. cat. (Rome, 1991).

C. Villa, *Le strade consolari di Roma* (Rome, 1995).

Noteworthy studies of specific geographical areas, but also containing a broad range of information of a general nature, include:

A. Grenier, *Le strade romane della Gallia* (Ital. trans., Rome, 1937).

D. Sterpos, *Le strade romane in Italia. Quaderni di Autostrade*, 17 (Rome, 1969). (Also: *The Roman Roads in Italy* [Rome, 1970].)

L. Quilici, *Le strade. Viabilità tra Roma e Lazio. Vita e costumi dei romani antichi*, 12. (Rome, 1990).

A series of monograph studies was also published in the collection "Atlante tematico di topografia romana," L. Quilici and S. Quilici Gigli, eds. (Bretschneider, Rome). Thus far, these include the following volumes:

1. *Tecnica stradale romana*, 1992; 2. *Strade romane: Percorsi e infrastrutture*, 1993; and 5. *Strade romane: Ponti e viadotti*, 1996.

Index